First World War
and Army of Occupation
War Diary
France, Belgium and Germany

29 DIVISION
Headquarters, Branches and Services
General Staff
1 August 1916 - 31 August 1916

WO95/2280/5

The Naval & Military Press Ltd
www.nmarchive.com
Published in association with The National Archives

Published by

The Naval & Military Press Ltd

Unit 10 Ridgewood Industrial Park,

Uckfield, East Sussex,

TN22 5QE England

Tel: +44 (0) 1825 749494

www.naval-military-press.com

www.nmarchive.com

This diary has been reprinted in facsimile from the original. Any imperfections are inevitably reproduced and the quality may fall short of modern type and cartographic standards.

© **Crown Copyright**
Images reproduced by permission of The National Archives, London, England, 2015.

Miscellaneous	Special Report On Shells Used By The Enemy At 23.00 (And In The Intelligence Report Of The 8th August, Wrongly Described As Rifle Grenades.		
Miscellaneous	29th Division Daily Intelligence Summary. From 10 a.m. 6/8/16 to 10 a.m. 7/8/16	06/08/1916	06/08/1916
Miscellaneous	29th Division Daily Intelligence Summary. From 10 a.m. 5.8.16. to 10 a.m. 6.8.16	05/08/1916	05/08/1916
Miscellaneous	29th Division Daily Intelligence Summary. From 10 a.m. 4.8.16. to 10 a.m. 5.8.16	04/08/1916	04/08/1916
Miscellaneous	29th Division Daily Intelligence Summary. From 10 a.m. 3.8.16. to 10 a.m. 4.8.16	03/08/1916	03/08/1916
Miscellaneous	29th Division Daily Intelligence Summary. From 12 Noon 2.8.16. to 12 Noon 3.8.16	02/08/1916	02/08/1916
Miscellaneous	29th Division Daily Intelligence Summary. From 12 Noon 1.8.16 to 12 Noon 2.8.16	01/08/1916	01/08/1916
Miscellaneous	29th Division. Intelligence Summary	01/08/1916	01/08/1916
Miscellaneous	29th Division Weekly Operations Report. Period From 6 p.m. 3.8.16. to 6 p.m. 10.8.16	03/08/1916	03/08/1916
Miscellaneous	29th Division Summary Of Operation	03/08/1916	03/08/1916
Miscellaneous	29th Division Weekly Summary. Operations.	17/08/1916	17/08/1916
Miscellaneous	29th Division Weekly Operation Report.	24/08/1916	24/08/1916
Miscellaneous	29th Division Weekly Operation Report. App 6	31/08/1916	31/08/1916

Miscellaneous	Work Report 29th Division Period ending 13/8/16	14/08/1916	14/08/1916
Miscellaneous	Work Report. 29th Division Period Ending 6/8/16	09/08/1916	09/08/1916
Miscellaneous	29th Division Daily Summary. From 10 a.m. 31.8.16. to 10 a.m. 1.9.16. App 5	31/08/1916	31/08/1916
Miscellaneous	29th Division Daily Summary. From 10 a.m. 30.8.16. to 10 a.m. 31.8.16	30/08/1916	30/08/1916
Miscellaneous	29th Division Daily Summary. From 10 a.m. 29.8.16. to 10 a.m. 30.8.16	29/08/1916	29/08/1916
Miscellaneous	29th Division Daily Summary From 10 a.m. 28.8.16 to 10 a.m. 29.8.16	28/08/1916	28/08/1916
Miscellaneous	29th Division Daily Summary. From 10 a.m. 27.8.16. to 10 a.m. 28.8.16	27/08/1916	27/08/1916
Miscellaneous	29th Division Daily Summary. From 10 a.m. 26.8.16 to a.m. 27.8.16	26/08/1916	26/08/1916
Miscellaneous	29th Division Daily Summary. From 10 a.m. 25.8.16 to 10 a.m. 26.8.16	25/08/1916	25/08/1916
Miscellaneous	29th Division Daily Summary. From 10 a.m. 24.8.16 to 10 a.m. 25.8.16	24/08/1916	24/08/1916
Miscellaneous	29th Division Daily Summary. From 10 a.m. 23.8.16 to 10 a.m. 24.8.16	23/08/1916	23/08/1916
Miscellaneous	29th Division Daily Summary. From 10 a.m. 22.8.16. to 10 a.m. 23.8.16	22/08/1916	22/08/1916
Miscellaneous	29th Division Daily Summary. From 10 a.m. 21.8.16. to 10 a.m. 22.8.16	21/08/1916	21/08/1916
Miscellaneous	29th Division Daily Summary. From 10 a.m. 20.8.16. to 10 a.m. 21.8.16	20/08/1916	20/08/1916
Miscellaneous	List of Articles Found on a dead german Soldier at C 29. d. 1.0 Night 20/21 August 1916		
Miscellaneous	29th Division Daily Summary. From 10 a.m. 19.8.16. to 10 a.m. 19.8.16. to 10 a.m. 20.8.16	19/08/1916	19/08/1916
Miscellaneous	29th Division Daily Summary From 10 a.m. 18.8.16 to 10 a.m. 19.8.16	18/08/1916	18/08/1916
Miscellaneous	29th Division Daily Summary. From 10 a.m. 17.8.16. to 10 a.m. 18.8.16	17/08/1916	17/08/1916
Miscellaneous	29th Division Daily Summary. From 10 a.m. 16.8.16. to 10 a.m. 17.8.16	16/08/1916	16/08/1916
Miscellaneous	29th Division Daily Summary. From 10 a.m. 15.8.16. to 10 a.m. 16.8.16	15/08/1916	15/08/1916
Miscellaneous	29th Division Daily Summary. From 10 a.m. 14.8.16. to 10 a.m. 15.8.16.	14/08/1916	14/08/1916
Miscellaneous	Intelligence. VIIIth Corps.	15/08/1916	15/08/1916
Miscellaneous	29th Division Daily Summary. From 10 a.m. 13.8.16. to 10 a.m. 14.8.16.	13/08/1916	13/08/1916
Miscellaneous	29th Division Daily Summary. From 10 a.m. 12.8.16. to a.m. 13.8.16.	12/08/1916	12/08/1916
Miscellaneous	29th Division Daily Summary. From 10 a.m. 11.8.16. to 10 a.m. 12.8.16	11/08/1916	11/08/1916
Miscellaneous	29th Division Daily Summary. From 10 a.m. 10.8.16. to 10 a.m. 11.8.16.	10/08/1916	10/08/1916
Miscellaneous	29th Division Daily Summary. From 10 a.m. 9.8.16. to 10 a.m. 10.8.16.	09/08/1916	09/08/1916
Miscellaneous	29th Division Daily Intelligence Summary. From 10. a.m. 8.8.16 to 10. a.m. 9.8.16.	08/08/1916	08/08/1916
Miscellaneous	29th Division Daily Intelligence Summary. From 10 a.m. 7.8.16. to 10 a.m. 8.8.16	07/08/1916	07/08/1916

Contents

Document type	Place/Title	Date From	Date To
Heading	War Diary General Staff 29th Division August 1916		
Heading	War Diary General Staff 29th Division For August 1916 Volume XVIII		
War Diary		01/08/1916	31/08/1916
Miscellaneous	Report On The Enemy Gas Attack On Night Of 8/9th August 1916.	09/08/1916	09/08/1916
Miscellaneous	Cases Of Drift Gas Poisoning.	09/08/1916	09/08/1916
Miscellaneous	Cases Of Drift Gas Poisoning.		
Miscellaneous	Notes On Report By 29th Division Of The Gas Attack On The Night Of August 8th/9th, 1916		
Miscellaneous	Corps Commander's Remarks On Report By 29th Division Of The Gas Attack August 8/9th		
Miscellaneous	App 1 (a)		
Miscellaneous	Machine Gun Action On July 1st.		
Miscellaneous	From Officer Commanding 88th Machine Gun Coy		
Miscellaneous	Reliefs August 1916 29th Div App 1 (b)		
Miscellaneous	Report On The Enemy Gas Attack On Night Of 8/9th August 1916. App 1 (e)		
Miscellaneous	29th Division Conference No. 10 Held On 12th August, 1916. App 1 (d)	19/08/1916	19/08/1916
Miscellaneous	Report On Gas Discharge On 29th Division Front On Night Of 31st August/1st September. App 1 (e)		
Miscellaneous	29th Division Dispositions-2nd August, 1916. App 2 (a)	02/08/1916	02/08/1916
Miscellaneous	29th Division-Location Of Units-5-8-16. App 2 (b)	05/08/1916	05/08/1916
Miscellaneous	29th Division-Location Of Units-12th August. 1916. App 2 (c)		
Miscellaneous	29th Division-Location Of Units-At 9 A.M. 19th August 1916 (d).		
Miscellaneous	29th Division-Location Of Units-20th August, 1916. App 2 (e)	20/08/1916	20/08/1916
Miscellaneous	29th Division-Location Of Units-26th August, 1916 App 2 (c)	26/08/1916	26/08/1916
Miscellaneous	29th Division-Location Of Units-31st August, 1916. App 2 (g)	31/08/1916	31/08/1916
Miscellaneous	29th Division Operation Order No. 53. App. 3 (a)		
Miscellaneous			
Operation(al) Order(s)	29th Division Operation Order No. 54. App 3 (b)		
Miscellaneous	Table Of Moves.		
Miscellaneous	29th Division Order No. 55. App 3 (c)		
Miscellaneous	Appendix. 86th Brigade.		
Miscellaneous	Correction To 29th Division Order No. 55	26/08/1916	26/08/1916
Operation(al) Order(s)	29th Division Order No. 56 App 3 (d)		
Miscellaneous	Moves Table.		
Operation(al) Order(s)	29th Division Order No. 57. App 3 (C)		
Miscellaneous	Amendment to 29th Division Order No. 57.	29/08/1916	29/08/1916
Operation(al) Order(s)	29th Division Order No. 38. app 3 (b)		
Miscellaneous	Headquarters. App 4.	31/08/1916	31/08/1916
Miscellaneous	Work Report-29th Division.	28/08/1916	28/08/1916
Miscellaneous	Work Report-29th Division.	24/08/1916	24/08/1916
Miscellaneous	Work Report. Right Sector.	17/08/1916	17/08/1916

Index..................

SUBJECT.

WAR DIARY

No.	Contents.	Date.

GENERAL STAFF
29th DIVISION

August
1916

Confidential

Vol 18

War Diary

General Staff
29th Division

for

August 1916

—

Volume XVIII

—

WAR DIARY – GENERAL STAFF, 29TH DIVISION.

August 1916

Army Form C. 2118.

AUGUST, 1916.

Place	Date	Hour	Summary of Events and Information	Remarks and references to Appendices
	August 1st.		Two Battalions 87th Brigade moved from CANAL BANK to relieve the 71st Brigade in the left sector trenches from DUKE STREET on the right to PRATT STREET inclusive on the left. Two Battalions 87th Brigade moved from PROVEN to CANAL BANK and YPRES. 87th Brigade Headquarters moved from PROVEN to RAMPARTS N. of MENIN ROAD. O.C. 87th Brigade took over command of left sector. (Appendix 3(k) July War-Diary). G.S.O.1 visited forward areas with G.S.O. 3, 65 Divn. G.O.C. visited Brigade Headquarters of 88th and 86th Brigades. Summaries of work carried out by Machine Guns of 86th, 87th and 88th Brigades during operations of 1st July is attached. Diagram shewing reliefs for the month of August is attached.	App.1(a) App.1(b)
	August 2nd		The G.S.O.II visited the left sector early. A demonstration of consolidation of a trench etc. was given at BERTHEN at 3 p.m., the G.O.C., G.S.O.I and III and Brigadier 86th Brigade attended, also 4 officers and 4 N.C.Os. from each Brigade. Army Commander visited 87: Bde at Camp C. Dispositions of the Division on this date is shewn in App.2(a).	App.2(a)

Army Form C. 2118.

WAR DIARY — GENERAL STAFF, 29TH DIVISION.

~~INTELLIGENCE SUMMARY.~~

(Erase heading not required.)

Instructions regarding War Diaries and Intelligence Summaries are contained in F. S. Regs., Part II. and the Staff Manual respectively. Title pages will be prepared in manuscript.

Place	Date	Hour	Summary of Events and Information	Remarks and references to Appendices
	August 3rd		The G.O.C., G.S.O.I and G.S.O.III all visited different sectors of the trenches, the G.S.O.I accompanying the Brigadier 86th Brigade and his Brigade Major. Capt. SWIFT, Royal Fusiliers, proceeded to the Training School, ROUEN, to replace Capt. FARRELL, Border Regiment, who was sent to England. A quiet day. Weather fine and very hot. The Divisional School opened at A.29.d.9.8. The previous class was reassembled for 10 days.	
	August 4th		A quiet day. The G.S.O.II visited the trenches of the right sector in the morning. A Corps Conference was held at 10 a.m. attended by the G.O.C., G.S.O.I, C.R.E. and Brigadiers. 2 Coys. of Pioneers and 2 sections R.E. from the 38th Division arrived in billets in YPRES for work under the 29th Division. B.G.G.S (VIII Corps), G.S.O.1 and CRE visited Ramparts and KRUIS Salient in the afternoon.	

WAR DIARY - GENERAL STAFF, 29TH DIVISION.

Army Form C. 2118.

~~INTELLIGENCE SUMMARY~~

(Erase heading not required.)

Instructions regarding War Diaries and Intelligence Summaries are contained in F. S. Regs., Part II. and the Staff Manual respectively. Title pages will be prepared in manuscript.

Place	Date	Hour	Summary of Events and Information	Remarks and references to Appendices
	August 5th		YPRES was shelled during the morning. The G.O.C. visited the right sector trenches early. G.S.O.II went to 87th Brigade Headquarters and to the 2 machine guns East of POTIJZE which were registered on the German trenches East of RAILWAY WOOD. Disposition of the Division on this date is shown in App.2(b).	App.2(b)
	August 6th		The G.S.O.I visited right sector trenches in the early morning. G.S.O.III visited left trenches later, and the G.S.O.II went round some of the machine gun emplacements with the O.C. 88th Machine Gun Coy. in the afternoon. A quiet day. Appointment of Capt. HICKES as G.S.O.III not approved.	

Army Form C. 2118.

WAR DIARY - GENERAL STAFF, 29TH DIVISION.

INTELLIGENCE SUMMARY.

(Erase heading not required.)

Instructions regarding War Diaries and Intelligence Summaries are contained in F. S. Regs., Part II. and the Staff Manual respectively. Title pages will be prepared in manuscript.

Place	Date	Hour	Summary of Events and Information	Remarks and references to Appendices
	August 7th		The G.O.C. went to the trenches of the right sector early. The G.S.O.III visited the right sector trenches with Major CLARKE (attached to the Division G.S.) to show him round. The G.S.O.II visited LA BRIQUE and ST. JEAN in the evening, to consider best method of defence of former post and visit Machine gun emplacements. A Division course of bombing commenced at Camp C.	
	August 8th		The G.O.C. went round the trenches of the right sector with Brig-General CAYLEY in the morning. The G.S.O.III and Major CLARKE visited the right sector later. Major CLARKE and right & our left Brigade, took over duties from Capt. HICKES. At 10.30 p.m. the enemy gassed the left Battalion of our right Brigade, but did not attempt to attack, he also bombarded our front trenches and support trenches but not very severely; a special report on this subject is attached as App.1(c). We had several casualties; the effects of the gas was felt some 12 hours after the discharge although at the time the men felt nothing. 86th Brigade relieved 87th Brigade in the left sector on the nights 8th/9th & 9th/10th Operation Order No.53 (App.3(a))	App.1(c) App.3(a)

WAR DIARY - GENERAL STAFF, 29TH DIVISION.

Army Form C. 2118.

~~INTELLIGENCE~~ ~~SUMMARY~~

(Erase heading not required.)

Place	Date	Hour	Summary of Events and Information	Remarks and references to Appendices
	August 9th		The G.S.O.II visited the Machine Gun emplacements in the right sector. The G.S.O.III inspected the Divisional O.P. in the left sector. The G.O.C. went round the Train and Transport lines in the morning. Capt. HICKES rejoined the 29th Divisional Artillery at BERTRANCOURT. Army Commander visited G.O.C at 4 p.m at April 145th	
	August 10th		The G.O.C. visited POTIJZE and LA BRIQUE defences early. The G.S.O.I visited KAAIE Salient defences etc.	

WAR DIARY - GENERAL STAFF, 29TH DIVISION.

Army Form C. 2118.

Place	Date	Hour	Summary of Events and Information	Remarks and references to Appendices
	August 11th		The G.S.O.II visited the left trenches of the right sector early. A battalion (the 14th Welsh Regt.) was sent to be attached to 29th Division for cable burying work; it was billeted at BRANDHOEK. Several deaths due to gas poisoning occurred during the day. The Germans made a small raid on our trenches just South of GULLY about midnight 11/12th only one German got to our trench and he was killed, the remainder only succeeded in reaching our wire, our casualties were 1 officer and 1 sergeant killed.	
	August 12th		The total number of casualties due to gas have now risen to 25 officers and 365 other ranks made up as follows - Killed 11 officers 117 other ranks - wounded 14 officers 248 other ranks. The G.O.C. accompanied the Corps Commander round the left sector trenches at 5.30 a.m. At 10 a.m. the G.O.C. inspected the Divisional School on termination of the course, the Corps Commander was present. The G.S.O.II visited the trenches of the left sector with the A.A. & Q.M.G. in the afternoon. The G.S.O.I went to see the work being done in the trenches in left sector at night. Capt. AINSLIE came to Divisional Headquarters as understudy to G.S.O.III. Disposition of the Division on this date is shewn in App.2(c). A conference was held at ~~Divisional~~ Headquarters on this date (App.1(d)) at Camp C. Reserve Bde	App.2(c) App.1(d)

WAR DIARY - GENERAL STAFF, 29TH DIVISION.

(Erase heading not required.)

Army Form C. 2118.

Instructions regarding War Diaries and Intelligence Summaries are contained in F. S. Regs., Part II. and the Staff Manual respectively. Title pages will be prepared in manuscript.

Place	Date	Hour	Summary of Events and Information	Remarks and references to Appendices
	August 13th		A quiet day. A Corps Conference took place at Corps Headquarters at 2 p.m. and was attended by the G.O.C. G.S.O.I, A.A. & Q.M.G., C.R.A., C.R.E. and all Brigadiers. Weather still fine.	
	August 14th		The G.O.C. visited the right sector trenches early. H.M. the KING accompanied by the PRINCE of WALES visited the Divisional Headquarters at 4 p.m. and was introduced to the Brigadiers, C.R.A., G.S.O.I and A.A. & Q.M.G., the G.O.C.4th Division and his Brigadiers were also present and were introduced. His Majesty left about 4.45 p.m. after tea. The G.S.O.II and Divisional Bombing Officer went to the Second Army Infantry School, WISQUES, to attend a lecture by Capt. BROTHERS (Canadian Division) on bombing. A quiet day.	

WAR DIARY - GENERAL STAFF, 29TH DIVISION.

Place	Date	Hour	Summary of Events and Information	Remarks and references to Appendices
	August 15th		The G.S.O.II and Capt. AINSLIE reconnoitred the emergency track for wheeled traffic from C. Camp to Bridge 4 over the Canal N. of YPRES; it was not possible to travel the whole distance in a car, the track was narrow and bad and very difficult to find; they afterwards inspected the KAAIE Salient trenches. The G.O.C. visited A and C Camps in the morning. The G.S.O.I visited H.Q. of forward Brigades in evening, and L.4 and L.8 works. The G.S.O.III visited the Intelligence Officers of the forward Brigades with the G.S.O.III Corps Intelligence in the afternoon. During the early hours of the morning a hostile aeroplane dropped a few bombs on the main YPRES - POPERINGHE Road; it also opened fire with a machine gun. No damage was done. A quiet day. Strong south wind.	
	August 16th		The G.O.C. and G.S.O.I visited the southern part of the 4th Division trenches and our trenches about WIELTJE early in the morning. The G.S.O.III and Capt. AINSLIE reconnoitred PICCADILLY and neighbouring trenches during the afternoon. The G.S.O.II visited PARADISE ALLEY and WIELTJE at night with the O.C. 177th Tunnelling Coy. and the O.C. 86th Machine Gun Coy. to decide on Machine Gun emplacements, for strong points at these places. There was some rain during the night 16th/17th. Work proceeded on the trench connecting WIELTJE with NEW JOHN STREET.	

WAR DIARY - GENERAL STAFF, 29TH DIVISION.

INTELLIGENCE SUMMARY.

(Erase heading not required.)

Place	Date	Hour	Summary of Events and Information	Remarks and references to Appendices
	August 17th		At about 2.45 a.m. a false gas alarm was given owing to a man mistaking the words "Gas alert on" for "Gas alarm", it was however immediately cancelled, but not before our artillery had opened a barrage on the enemy's front line, which had the good effect of causing casualties amongst an enemy working party opposite our right trenches. The G.O.C. visited some of the L and P line defended points in the afternoon. The G.S.O.III visited the Brigade and Battalion H.Q. in YPRES and on Canal Bank. From information received it appears that the enemy are again inserting gas cylinders opposite the 4th Division Front near the Canal. Wind S.W. Several showers occurred during the day.	
	August 18th		The G.O.C. visited the trenches early accompanied by the Brigadier 86th Brigade; he inspected WIELTJE and the new trench to NEW JOHN STREET, he then went along the front line to RAILWAY WOOD. G.S.O.I visited Railway Wood trenches in the morning. The G.S.O.II went to the trenches about White Chateau in the afternoon. There was a heavy rain storm in the afternoon. 2 Battalions 87th Brigade moved to YPRES and CANAL BANK in relief of 2 Battalions 86th Brigade which relieved 2 Battalions of 88th Brigade in right sector front trenches. Machine Gun Coys. also changed over. 2 Battalions 88th Brigade moved to Divisional Reserve in A.B.C.O. Camps. vide Operation Order No.54 (App.3(b)) G.O.C, G.S.O.I, CRA, CRE and arty Bde Commanders attended a Conference at Corps H.Qrs at 2.30 p.m.	App. 3(b)

WAR DIARY – GENERAL STAFF, 29TH DIVISION.

Army Form C. 2118.

~~INTELLIGENCE SUMMARY~~

(Erase heading not required.)

Instructions regarding War Diaries and Intelligence Summaries are contained in F. S. Regs., Part II. and the Staff Manual respectively. Title pages will be prepared in manuscript.

Place	Date	Hour	Summary of Events and Information	Remarks and references to Appendices
	August 19th		G.S.O.II visited the left trenches and ENGLISH FARM early. The G.O.C. went to WISQUES early to see the Second Army Central School. Heavy rain during the morning. During the night 19th/20th 2 Battalions 87th Brigade moved from YPRES and CANAL BANK to trenches in relief of 2 Battalions 88th Brigade which moved to YPRES in reserve to right sector replacing 2 Battalions 88th Brigade which moved to Divisional Reserve in A.B.C.O. Camps. H.Q. 86th Brigade moved to Right Brigade H.Q. H.Q. 88th Brigade moved to C. Camp. 12th Brigade of 4th Division on our left was relieved by 114th Brigade of 38th (Welsh) Division. Disposition of the Division on this date is shewn in App.2(d).	App. 3(b) App.2(d)
	August 20th		A very quiet day. The G.O.C. reconnoitred ground round C. Camp with a view to selecting a suitable winter training ground for the Reserve Brigade. G.S.O.I and II visited the Reigersburg (4.10 in the afternoon. Disposition of the Division on this date is shewn in App.2(e).	App.2(e)

WAR DIARY - GENERAL STAFF, 29TH DIVISION.

INTELLIGENCE SUMMARY

(Erase heading not required.)

Place	Date	Hour	Summary of Events and Information	Remarks and references to Appendices
	August 21st		The G.O.C. visited the right and centre trenches early. A quiet morning. At 3 p.m. the VIIIth Corps H.A. and 20th Divisional Artillery carried out a bombardment of the German front trenches for about 2 hours from C.29.central to Canadian Dugouts. 200 9.2" shells and 300 6" shells were fired by the H.A. with a view to smashing the suspected enemy's gas cylinders. G.S.O.1 visited English Farm, Gunyere walk and Potijze. At 8.30 p.m. "GAS" was received from the left Brigade, but it afterwards turned out to be a false alarm, (which had been started by the Right Division.) Wind north and slight.	
	August 22nd		The G.S.O.II visited the trenches of the right sector early. The G.O.C. visited the training of the Reserve (88th) Brigade in Camp. A quiet day. Wind slight north-west. The "Gas Alert" was put "ON".	

WAR DIARY - GENERAL STAFF, 29TH DIVISION.

Army Form C. 2118.

Place	Date	Hour	Summary of Events and Information	Remarks and references to Appendices
	August 23rd		The G.O.C. and G.S.O.III visited the left trenches and the Divisional N. O.P. early. The G.S.O.I inspected the gas cylinder emplacements in right sector; the C.R.E. also inspected these emplacements, orders having been received that we are to be prepared to insert cylinders as soon as possible. The G.S.O.II visited 2 Machine Gun emplacements in CONGREVE WALK and PAGODA CORNER in the afternoon. The G.S.O.III and Divisional Gas Officer attended a lecture on GAS by a French officer at the Second Army School, WISQUES, at 6 p.m. The G.O.C. and G.S.O.II went to dine with the G.O.C. 3rd Canadian Division; the Corps Commander was present, and the question of mutual Machine gun support between the 29th and 3rd Canadian Division on our right was discussed.	
	August 24th		The G.O.C. went round the trenches with the O.C. London Field Coy. early. The G.S.O.II and Brigade Majors of all Brigades went to a lecture on Raids and aeroplane photography by a Canadian Officer near ABEELE at 10 a.m.	

WAR DIARY - GENERAL STAFF, 29TH DIVISION.

Army Form C. 2118.

Instructions regarding War Diaries and Intelligence Summaries are contained in F. S. Regs., Part II. and the Staff Manual respectively. Title pages will be prepared in manuscript.

(Erase heading not required.)

Place	Date	Hour	Summary of Events and Information	Remarks and references to Appendices
	August 25th		A lecture was given at the Divisional School by Capt. BROTHERS, 1st Canadian Division, to all bombing officers and N.C.Os., to the bombing class under the Divisional Grenadier officer, and to the Divisional School and other officers at 10 a.m. The G.O.C. attended the lecture. A quiet day. *G.S.O.1 visited Bde H.Qrs in YPRES in the afternoon.* The 14th Welsh Regiment who had been assisting us burying cables were taken from us and we had to provide 400 men from our reserve Brigade for the purpose during the night 25th/26th. (App.3(c)). Operation Order No.55 containing instructions re installation of gas cylinders was issued	App.3(c)
	August 26th		Capt. AINSLIE (understudy to G.S.O.III) left for G.H.Q. on appointment as an instructor at the G.H.Q. Training School. The G.O.C. and G.S.O.I separately visited the trenches early. The Corps Commander visited the Divisional School at 3 p.m. and afterwards witnessed the 88th Brigade Assault at Arms for a short time. The reserve Brigade (88th) provided 800 men during the night 26th/27th for cable burying. Work is proceeding with the construction of gas cylinder emplacements. Amendment to Operation Order No.55 issued (App.3(c)). Disposition of the Division on this date is shewn in App.2(f).	App.3(c) App.2(f)

WAR DIARY - GENERAL STAFF, 29TH DIVISION.

Army Form C. 2118.

Place	Date	Hour	Summary of Events and Information	Remarks and references to Appendices
	August 27th		During the morning the G.O.C. held a conference with Battalion Commanders of 88th Brigade with reference to work in the trenches. Work was continued on the gas cylinder emplacements and 196 cylinders were installed during the night 27th/28th vide 29th Division O.O. No.55 A quiet day. G.S.O.1 took G.O.C. Major down to Bde HQrs in YPRES in the afternoon. The G.S.O.III and A.A. & Q.M.G. visited the right sector trenches in the afternoon and the G.S.O.III was present on the arrival of the gas cylinder lorries at POTIJZE and MENIN ROAD at 10 p.m. and onwards. Operation Order No.56 regarding relief of 86th Brigade by 88th Brigade in the right sector was issued (App.3(d)).	App. 3(c) App. 3(d)
	August 28th		The G.O.C. and the Corps Commander went round the left sector trenches early. The Army Commander visited the 86th and 87th Brigade Headquarters at YPRES at 8.15 and 8.30 a.m. respectively. The G.S.O.I visited the trenches with the C.R.E. early. (Right Sector) The G.O.C., G.S.O.I and Commandant Divisional School visited a demonstration at the Second Army School at WISQUES during the afternoon, (consolidation of a crater etc.). 164 gas cylinders were carried up to the trenches on night of 28th/29th. The G.S.O.II saw that all arrangements worked satisfactorily. Orders for gas discharge were issued vide Operation Order No.57 (App.3(e)).	App. 3(e)

Army Form C. 2118.

WAR DIARY - GENERAL STAFF, 29TH DIVISION.

INTELLIGENCE SUMMARY.

(Erase heading not required.)

Instructions regarding War Diaries and Intelligence Summaries are contained in F.S. Regs., Part II. and the Staff Manual respectively. Title pages will be prepared in manuscript.

Place	Date	Hour	Summary of Events and Information	Remarks and references to Appendices
	August 29th		A lecture was given to the Divisional School and 150 officers and other ranks of 88th Brigade on bayonet fighting by Capt. BETTS (from Second Army School of Instruction) at 10 a.m. The G.O.C. and G.S.O.I attended it. The G.S.O.II, D.A.D.M.S. and Divisional Gas Officer attended a course at the Second Army Gas School at OXELAERE at 10.30 a.m. on the new gas box respirator shortly to be issued in place of P.H.G. helmets. During the night 29th/30th, 2 Battalions 88th Brigade moved from C. Camp to trenches right sector in relief of 2 Battalions of 86th Brigade who moved to C. Camp. (App.3(d)). Gas was to have been emitted at 1.30 a.m. night 29th/30th, but the wind was not favourable. The 88th M.G. Coy. relieved that of the 86th Machine Gun Coy. Amendment to Operation Order No.57 issued on this date (App.3(e)). G.O.C, G.S.O.I, CRA and adj Bde Commanders attended a Conference at Corps HQrs at 2.30 p.m.	App.3(d) App.3(e)
	August 30th		There was heavy rain during the night 29th/30th and all day the 30th, and a northerly gale in afternoon. The G.S.O.II visited the right sector trenches (RAILWAY WOOD) in afternoon, the trenches were comparatively dry. The G.S.O.I visited REIGERSBERG defended post in the evening. During the night 30/31st 2 Battalions 88th Brigade from C. Camp relieved 2 Battalions 86th Brigade in YPRES. G.O.C. 88th Brigade took over command of the Right Sector. Further orders re gas discharge were issued (App.3(f)).	App.3(f)

Army Form C. 2118.

WAR DIARY - GENERAL STAFF, 29TH DIVISION.
~~INTELLIGENCE SUMMARY~~
(Erase heading not required.)

Instructions regarding War Diaries and Intelligence Summaries are contained in F. S. Regs., Part II. and the Staff Manual respectively. Title pages will be prepared in manuscript.

Place	Date	Hour	Summary of Events and Information	Remarks and references to Appendices
	August 31st		The G.O.C. visited the whole front. The G.S.O.I and C.R.E. also visited the trenches (centre and left sectors). A fine day day. A great deal of work was done on drainage of trenches. GAS was emitted from our right sector (RAILWAY WOOD) at 1.30 a.m. night of 31st/1st but the wind was not favourable for our left sector, so it was reserved. Two patrols from RAILWAY WOOD were sent out after the gas discharge and ascertained that the effects were felt by the enemy, they heard sounds of coughing and of fanning of trenches etc. A special report on the gas attack is attached to App. 1(e)	App. 1(e)
			Disposition of the Division on this date is shewn in App.2(f). Reports on work carried out during the month are attached as App.4. Daily Summaries 1st to 31st August are attached as App.5. Weekly Operation Reports for the month of August are attached as App.6.	App.2(f) App.4 App.5 App.6

Signed S. Fuller
Lt.Col. G.S.
29. Division.

REPORT ON THE ENEMY GAS ATTACK ON NIGHT OF

8/9th AUGUST 1916.

1. A gas attack by the enemy took place last night on the centre of the front held by this Division.
   The total front affected by the gas discharge was from A 1. to A 7. but the gas appears to have been heaviest opposite the following two sections of the line.
   A 1 - A 5.
   A 7 - part of A 8.
held by the left Battalion of the Right Brigade, and left Company of the right Battalion of the Left Brigade respectively, among whom (especially the latter) the casualties were severe.

2. The gas alarm was sounded at 10.30 pm., when the gas cloud came rapidly over our trenches. It tavelled about 1000 yards in ten minutes. The men in some cases had not time to put on their helmets although the alarm was taken up along the line immediately the presence of gas was detected, and gongs and Strombos Horns sounded.

3. The bombing and Lewis Gun post of the right Battalion (Right Brigade) on the railway, about I.11.b.67, reported that they heard a hissing sound to their left, though no gas actually passed over their lines.
   The gas appears to have been emitted in two clouds, but the interval of time between the discharges cannot be ascertained.

4. The enemy bombarded the front trenches from A.5.a. to A 8. very heavily, and damaged the parapet in several places.
   It seems probable that he intended to raid our trenches in this locality, but the heavy Lewis gun fire maintained by the garrison of these trenches on the German front line, together with enfilade machine gun fire from RAILWAY WOOD, and the artillery barrage, which was promptly applied, frustrated any such attempt, and the enemy did not leave his trenches.

5. The gas clouds were very dense for about half an hour, and hung about for a considerable time afterwards.
   The clouds were very local in their effect, and travelled West by South as although the troops between H 15 - H 20 did not detect any gas, the troops and Battalion Headquarters in F 13 felt the effect.
   The Battalion Headquarters at POTIJZE hardly discerned the gas, but in YPRES behind the Ramparts, especially South of the MENIN Road, the cloud was very noticeable.

6. Helmets could be removed with safety at 12.30 am. and at 1.0 am, working parties and wiring parties in front of our trenches on the right of the Line resumed their work.

7. The gas travelled exceptionally far, as the cloud presumably from the 4th Division Area, reached Divisional Headquarters at A.25.d.1.4. a distance of nearly 13000 yards about 11.0 pm., and necessitated gas helmets being worn. This cloud was so local in its affect that the horse lines of the Headquarters and of the R.E. situated some 100 yards on either flank were not inconvenienced.

8. I append a list of the casualties from gassing reported up to date. They were, I regret to say, severe due to the suddenness of the attack, and thenspeed at which the gas

travelled.   This is the first time this Division has
experienced a gas attack, and this accounts for a proportion of
the casualties, due to the men removing their helmets before the
gas clouds had dispersed.
　　　　　　The troops behaved very well under trying circumstances
and the names of several officers have been brought to my
notice for good work.

9. "Gas alert" had been ordered by both Brigades last night.

　　　　　　　　　　　　　　　　Major General.
9th August 1916.　　　　　　　Commanding 29th Division.

CASES OF DRIFT GAS POISONING.

	Officers.	Other Ranks.
1st K.O.S.B.		9
1st Royal Inniskilling Fus. .	4	60
2nd Hampshire Regt.	3	27
88th Machine Gun Coy.		2
1st West Riding R.E.		1
88th T.M. Battery		1
	7	80

Officers — 2nd Hampshire Regt.

2nd Lieut. SMITH, M.T.
  "   "   McCURDY, G. (Died)
Capt.   VICARS-MILES, L.W.
Lieut. TURNER. (Died)

1st R. Inniskilling Fus.

2nd Lieut. FIELD, S.H. (Died)
  "   "   DAVIDSON, G.L.
  "   "   ELVIDGE, L. (Died)
  "   "   FLETCHER, G.W.

Units other than 29th Division.

177th Tunnelling Co. R.E..........	3
19th Welsh Pioneers	5
151 Field Co. R.E.	1
1st Hants. Regt.	2
	11

Deaths.

	Other Ranks.
West Riding R.E.	1
1st Royal Inniskilling Fus.	23
2nd Hampshire Regt.	10
	34

travelled. This is the first time this Division has experienced a gas attack, and this accounts for a proportion of the casualties, due to the men removing their helmets before the gas clouds had dispersed.

The troops behaved very well under trying circumstances and the names of several officers have been brought to my notice for good work.

9. "Gas ~~Alert~~ Alert" had been ordered by both Brigades last night.

9th August 1916.

(Sd) H. de B. de Lisle.
Major General.
Commanding 29th Division.

CASES OF DRIFT GAS POISONING.

	Officers.	Other Ranks.
1st K.O.S.B.		9
1st Royal Inniskilling Fus. .	4	60
2nd Hampshire Regt.	3	27
88th Machine Gun Coy.		2
1st West Riding R.E.		1
88th T.M. Battery		1
	7	80

Officers   2nd Hampshire Regt.

2nd Lieut. SMITH, M.T.
 "   "   McCURDY, G. (Died)
Capt.   VICARS-MILES, L.W.
Lieut. TURNER. (Died)

1st R. Inniskilling Fus.

2nd Lieut. FIELD, S.H. (Died)
 "   "   DAVIDSON, G.L.
 "   "   ELVIDGE, L. (Died)
 "   "   FLETCHER, G.W.

Units other than 29th Division.

177th Tunnelling Co. R.E.	3
19th Welsh Pioneers	5
151 Field Co. R.E.	1
1st Hants. Regt.	2
	11

Deaths.

	Other Ranks.
West Riding R.E.	1
1st Royal Inniskilling Fus.	23
2nd Hampshire Regt.	10
	34

NOTES ON REPORT BY 29th DIVISION OF THE GAS ATTACK ON
THE NIGHT OF AUGUST 8th/9th, 1916.

****

General de Lisle stated the gas was let off at 10-30 p.m. from the Mound, and it came in two lots to the South-West and due West, affecting the left Company of the Hampshire Regiment and the left Company of the Inniskillings. The gas was seen coming over, and the strombos horns were going all along the line, and the general evidence is that there was heaps of time to put the masks on.

About 12-30 am August 9th (the time is rather vague) some people came from the support line up to the front line and said it was all over. They were not wearing masks at all and when the men in the front line saw this they took off their masks and some Officers went into their dug-outs before they were cleaned out with the sprayers. It appears the casualties occurred through the people taking off their masks too soon.

Early yesterday morning (August 9th) about 10 o'clock the casualties were more or less few, but later on a good many men who were perfectly alright felt a bit sick, got worse and were dead in 2 hours.

General de Lisle stated there was very little doubt in his mind that this gas contained a very large aamount of phosgene, and the majority of the men when they thought the gas was no longer so considerable took their masks off and then the gas took effect. Some men said their eyes began to water and they put their hands underneath their helmets to rub their eyes. Some men were on a working party without their coats on. One man in particular was ladling out some road repair material. He says he did not hear the strombos horn and did not know until the gas was on top of him. 12 horses were lost in the Division. The rats were lying dead all about the place, and on the first occasion the birds fell dead off the trees.

The general evidence is that the men had their masks on before the gas cloud came up, but with Phosgene gas the masks must be kept on for a considerable time afterwards.

General de Lisle's order to his Division is that the masks must not be removed until the order comes from the Battalion Commander, who will give the order on the recommendation of the Medical Officer.

There is very little doubt we had nearly three times as many casualties with the after effects than we had from the actual gas.

At 2-30pm yesterday the numbers given to the Army Commander were 7 Officers and about 90 men, but by 8 o'clock at night the numbers totalled up to about 300. A large number suffered with the after effects and a great number died. To quote a case : a C.S.M. of the Hampshires was perfectly alright at 8 o'clock yesterday morning, at 10 o'clock he was not feeling very well, and at 12 noon he was dead.

Some of the evidence shows that the enemy let off gas about 10-30pm and another lot at 11 o'clock, but whether this is correct or not is not known definitely. The evidence from the men who have been gassed is very vague.

The Brigadier commanding the 87th Brigade stated that so far as he could make out the left Company of the Inniskillings were all on the alert, but the Officers and N.C.O's got very little notice. They only got about 10-15 seconds notice that the gas was coming. They paid attention to the men getting their helmets on, and therefore all the Officers and all the best N.C.O's were died in about a couple of minutes..

The men wore their helmets for about $2\frac{1}{2}$ hours, and being pretty well exhausted took them off and laid down, some outside and some in the trench.

The vermoral sprayers were being used the whole of

the time, but with the number we had the trenches could not be absolutely cleared.

Most of the people in the left Company were killed straight away, but the right company was absolutely untouched. Yesterday, however, the whole of the right company began to be sick.

The question was raised as to whether the rations got tainted, and also the effect on the clothes. General Lucas stated that after about an hour he got quite sick from smelling his coat.

The men of the left Company died suddenly with no pain, and no foaming at the mouth, but those of the right company who subsequently died, suffered great pain, turned blue, and were foaming at the mouth.

It was suggested that all the strombus horns be taken out and fresh cylinders put in. Shell cases are perfectly useless.

It was pointed out that about 70 strombos horns per division were to be issued, viz:

        1 per 100 yds in the Front Line.
        1 " 200 " in the Support Line.
        1 " 400 " in the Reserve Line.

and a certain number behind, making a total of about 70 per Division.

It was stated that the strombos horns acted very well indeed.

The Corps Commander asked whether the sentries in each case were able to detect the gas and did they in each case sound the alarm and was that alarm successful. The answer was that individual sentries did see it and others did not.

The gas helmet was found to be effective. So far as the box respirators are concerned, no special enquiry has yet been made, but there were no casualties among the machine gunners. The box respirator appears to fail when you are unable to breathe through the nose.

An important point is that the men being exhausted

laid down at the bottom of the trench after taking their helmets off.

It was pointed out that everybody kept on working, taking the dead and dying away and also that the wiring parties continued. The Army Commander had stated that after a gas attack all work must cease until the following day.

Brigadier General Cayley stated that plenty of warning was given, and that many Platoon Officers had time to go round and see that the helmets were adjusted properly. As far as can be made out there were a certain number of casualties while the gas was going over but comparatively few. The greater number occurred after the men took their helmets off which was about 1 o'clock.

General de Lisle stated that the alarm reached his Headquarters about 11p.m. when the staff began to cough and their eyes began to water.

It was stated the rockets took a long time in lighting owing to dampness, which is a serious disadvantage.

It is an interesting fact that about 12 horses of the 29th Division were killed by the gas. There was a driver and two horses at "C" Camp which is about 11500 yards behind. One horse dropped down dead and the other was not affected. The Driver was only slightly affected and went to Hospital.

At the Divisional Headquarters, which is about 15500 yards behind they were obliged to put on their helmets and keep them on.

It was stated the Germans got out of their trenches by Kaiser Bill and laid down in the open, but did not come on at all. Our Lewis guns kept on firing.

CORPS COMMANDER'S REMARKS ON REPORT BY 29th DIVISION
OF THE GAS ATTACK AUGUST 8/9th.

Are the Vermoral Sprayers enough and do they effect their purpose with the new gas.

I do not think the sentries are in a position to detect detect the gas. A great number of the positions of the sentries are not too good; they cannot see anything at all.

Can anything be done for improving the method of wearing the masks.

Working parties without coats on. The coats of the men in the front system should not be taken off.

Suggested strings round the bottom of the helmet to tighten round the neck.

How long does the present gas mask last ?

More vermoral sprayers and also fans for getting the gas out of the trenches.

Phosgene has much more effect on people who take exertion. Question of men walking back to the Dressing Station.

To be ascertained from the Doctors - What length of time the helmets should be kept on.

How was the alarm sent and by what means did the alarm arrive at Company, Battalion, Brigade and Divisional Headquarters, and also the guns.

Necessity of having the rockets and means of ignition of rockets in water tight cases easily opened.

Is there any possible method of testing the air without breathing it ?

In a mixed gas of Chlorine and Phosgene does the Chlorine come back further than the Phosgene without being dissipated.

What effect has the Vermoral Sprayer on the Phosgene.

Is the food in the trenches (bread meat and milk) made poisonous by absorbing the gas either Chlorine or Phosgene.

Necessity of having telephones anywhere near the

front line in the dug-out of a responsible officer, and clear notices stating that every word said on the telephone can be heard by the enemy must be put up. The Artillery to be specially careful about this order.

Are occasional changes in the regularity of the programme of relief made.

The most dangerous time for a gas attack is when the men are coming up into the trenches and arrangements should be made whereby the helmets can be got on quickly.

The people who are the sentries of the Garrison should not pay more attention to the relief than the lookout towards the enemy. Similarly with the remainder of the garrison.

Did the machine guns reveal their positions to the enemy.

App 1 (a)

A short Summary of work done by the 86th Machine Gun Company during the recent operations:-

The 29th Division was ordered to take part in an attack on the German lines, in vicinity of Beaumont Hamel.

The area allotted to the 86th Brigade was about 1300 yards frontage.

Date of Attack. 1st July 1916. Time 7.30 a.m.

Employment of Guns

The Machine Guns of the 86th Brigade were situate in the forward system of trenches as follows:

No of Guns	Position	Approx: distance to Enemy
2	Bowery	1300 x
1	Pilk Street	800 x
1	Essex Str	800 x
1	Newtownards	450 x
1	"J" Street	300 x

The work allotted to these guns during the preliminary Bombardment, which lasted 7 days, was to fire intermittently during the night on the German front line and along the whole front of his wire, to prevent him repairing and making good the damage done during the day by our Artillery. At intervals during the night the guns were also employed to search the enemy's Communication trenches and to play on their Ration Roads.

Covering Fire

On the morning of the 1st July, The front line guns were increased to 8, the extra two being sent to the "Bowery".

At 10 minutes before Zero a barrage of Artillery and Machine Gun Fire was put on the enemy's front line, At this time a mine was exploded by us, and as soon as the debris had settled and under cover of our Fire 4 machine Guns entered the crater and established themselves on the forward lip, opening fire, 2 guns N and 2 guns S.

Degrees of Safety were used on all covering guns and as soon as our advancing Infantry came into view the guns were lifted on to the objective.

There is no doubt that this Covering fire was effective both in the advance and the subsequent retirement as throughout, no enemy Rifle fire was directed against our Infantry.

Protection of the Flanks.

Our flanks were well covered and protected by guns of the 13th Brigade on the N. and the 87th on the S. we in turn assisting the 13th & 87th up to the time of the assault.

Ammunition Supply

The System of supply was as follows:-
Forward S.A.A. Dumps had been established in the front line, In these Dumps there was in addition to S.A.A. Belt Boxes, Spareparts

Ammunition Supply (Continued)

Spare barrels, Belt filling Machines & Water & oil

All Transport men had been trained in rapidly filling belts.

Cartridges had been stripped from Bandoliers & Chargers placed in Specially marked Sandbags to facilitate rapid belt filling.

At each Dump under supervision of the Company Sergeant Major and two N.C.O's were parties of Ammunition carriers furnished by Units.

"Teams" going over the parapet Consisted of 1 N.C.O & 6 men (the two extra men were those attached from Units for training). The teams each carried the following Quantities of Ammunition.

1 N.C.O & 6 men each carried short length of Metallic Belt in Haversack (25 rds each belt) ——— 175 rds
N.C.O. ——— 1 Belt box ——— 250 "
Nos 1 & 2 ——— 1 " box each ——— 500 "
Nos 3, 4 & 6 2 " " " ——— 1500 "

Total taken over Parapet 2,345

Previous practice had been made in carrying this Quantity of Ammunition and it was found quite practicable.

The Company Reserve of 4,500 rounds per Gun (72,000) was loaded on four limbers, ready to move forward when ordered.

Old web slings were provided by D.A.D.O.S. for assisting in carrying two belt boxes per man.

Long Range Fire.	Long Range fire was carried out on the enemy's back system of trenches at ranges varying from 1500x to 2200x. It was found that by working by a Time table that at these long ranges good fire effect was obtained and it was easier to ensure that the fire was directed on the object desired.
Nature of Emplacements	All Emplacements were covered except "J" Street. The construction was roughly as follows. Dug into the sides of the slope of hill, so that the front of the emplacement conformed to the slope rendering it difficult for the enemy to pick up, during the whole of the Bombardment none of our Emplacements were hit. Heavy baulks of timber was used as supports, roof consisting of Iron Girders set close together, filled sandbags placed on the Girders, then sheets of Galvanised Iron to kept out the wet, then a layer of Chalk as a shell breaker, the whole being finally masked by sods. Recesses made in the sides of Emplacements and lined with wood taken from Boxes, formed suitable places for Belt Boxes, Water, Oil, Spare Barrel Cases, Extra barrels &c.
Water to Guns.	Empty Ammunition boxes form very suitable vessels for carrying water, and if the lid is replaced little or no water is wasted

Water (Continued)	in the carrying. Petrol tins are best when obtainable.
Oil Supply	No difficulty was experienced with oil, in addition to the oil contained in the Traversing Handle each man carried the ordinary oval oil bottle in his haversack (that supplied for use with Rifle ¼ pint); but it was found that the supply in the handles was more than sufficient for the day.
Spare Parts	In addition to the First Aid Case carried with each Gun, the following was carried in an extra Haversack supplied by D.A.D.O.S.

        Hammer
        Screwdriver
        Spanner
        Spare Muzzle Cup Attachment
        Cleaning rod

This was to obviate carrying the heavy spare part box in the first stage of the Attack.

Efficiency of the Guns.	Throughout the Preliminary Bombardment and the various stages of the attack the Guns as a whole were very efficient and gave little or no trouble. This is an interesting point, as N/10 of 16 guns formed part of the original Guns at the landing on the Gallipoli.
The Light Tripod	These were found to be of great service during the Attack as were the carrying handles.

In the Field
15th August 1916

E. Redfurth Captain.
Comdg. 86th Company Machine Gun Corps.

S E C R E T.

MACHINE GUN ACTION ON JULY 1st.

From 7-0 to 7.29.a.m. on July 1st. fire was opened on the German Front Line by the 8 Guns remaining under the orders of the O.C.,M.G.Coy.(Note. 8 guns had previously been attached to battalions and were under the orders of the Os.C.Battans. and advanced with them). The 8 remaining guns were to advance later, when required.

At 7-20.a.m. fire was lifted on to communication trenches between 1st and 2nd objectives until 7-30.a.m.

At 7-30.a.m.(hour for assault of 1st objective) fire was lifted on to 2nd objective. It had been previously decided that this covering fire should be maintained on 2nd objective, until 8-40.a.m. when Infantry would be advancing from 1st to 2nd objectives and had reached limit of safety.

When, however, the attack was held up in "No man's Land" and the German Wire, one gun opened fire on parties of Germans seen retreating down communication trenches. Another gun opened fire on Germans seen standing on their parapets and firing at our own troops lying in "No mans Land".

At this point it was useless to fire on 2nd objective (Range about 2300 yards) as it was known that our Infantry had not even reached 1st objective. At the same time it was impossible to keep up rapid fire on German front trenches owing to some of our troops having reached the German lines and the possibility of their being just behind these and under fire from our own guns though out of sight.

As regards covering fire, protection of flanks and long range fire, little can be said owing to the failure of the assault.

As regards Ammunition - It had been decided to take to take up with the guns the 14 belt boxes, in some cases slung over the shoulder with a strap, and in the pack on in some cases worn in the pack on the equipment and ~1400 loose rounds in packs.

It is considered that the carrying up of Reserve boxes of S.A.A. is inadvisable in the initial stages, ~~of~~ and the Machine Guns should rely on the Battalions for this should it be necessary.

7 Ammunition Carriers per gun were attached from Battalions.

The method adopted for distribution of guns, ammunition etc. carried in the attack was as follows:-

Each gun Team consisted of an N.C.O. and 5 men, with an additional detachment of 7 men per gun, the gun and ammunition was carried as follows:-

N.C.O.	2 Belt Boxes.
1.	Gun and light tripod, oil can.
2.	2 belt boxes, condenser, oil can.
3.	Spare parts box and pick.
4.	2 belt boxes.
5.	Tin of water (2 galls) and shovel.
6.	2 belt boxes and Range Finder.
7.8.9.	2 belt boxes.
10.	Heavy tripod.
11.12.	700 rounds each carried loose in pack.

Each man carried three sand bags. Extra water bottles taken if available.

"Confidential"

From Officer Commanding
88th Machine Gun Coy
To   The Brigade Major
     88th Brigade.

Subject   In The Field
Machine Gun Operations   Aug: 12th 1916

General

Reference your B.536 d/12/8/16.
There were no new lessons to be learnt from the recent operations as regards the employment of machine guns.

The enemy used the oldest established laws of machine gun tactics.

i. Control of approaches.
He had machine guns laid on the lanes in our wire.

ii. He reserved his fire.
He kept his machine guns in deep dug outs until our barrage had lifted and then placed them on the parapet with utter disregard for concealment.

iii. From a machine gun officer's point of view the advance could have been continued, with less casualties, by adopting the formation unsuitable to machine gun fire.

(a) Immediate deployment on coming under machine gun fire. and then advance

(b) In small numbers
(c) At irregular intervals
(d) In short rushes
(e) From different parts of the line

This has the advantage of confusing the machine gunner and he will not be able to maintain an organised offensive as he will not know from what direction or at what interval the next rush will take place with the result that he must keep altering his aim which will render his fire ineffective. Another reason for deployment from a machine gunner's point of view is the target will be changed from a concentrated to a linear target. The former is suitable for machine gun fire the latter unsuitable. Shallow formations during a temporary check are apt to cause crowding which is a favourable machine gun target.

2. Covering Fire — From 1500 yards in rear we engaged the enemy's front line. The results were good firing over our own front and support line troops. During the period of bombardment we kept the enemy's wire open from fire from the Yellow line at a range from 1500 – 1600 yds. The enemy was unable to repair his wire.

3. Flank Protection — During raids on the enemy's line we protected the flanks of our own troops by machine gun fire. The raiding frontage was defined and we enfiladed either side of it thus preventing the enemy from seeing what was happening and isolating the raiding frontage.

4. Long Range Fire — We stopped enemy transport from entering Beaumont Hamel by night by long range machine gun fire. The range used was from 1800 – 2,500 verified by independent witnesses of other units.

3.

5. Ammunition Supply.

The ammunition supply was a serious question. We went into action on July 1st with 4,500 rounds per gun. The normal supply was supplemented by ammunition carriers. Each man wore a distinctive mark (a red armlet) so as that he could get forward and backward without interference from the battle police. Forward ammunition dumps were established. The scheme worked satisfactorily.

6. Position of Machine guns in attack.

The 16 guns of my company were distributed as follows. Two guns were allotted to each attacking unit for its protection. These 2 guns were under the control of a M.G. officer. The 8 guns being under the command of a fire control commander. They were eight guns in reserve to follow 200 yards in rear of the reserve battalions at the disposal of the Brigade Commander to be used according to the tactical requirements of the situation.

7. Lesson Learnt.

Machine Guns should not accompany an assaulting force. They would be better employed affording covering fire from rear, to one's own advancing troops and go forward when the position is consolidated.

8. Casualties

We had no casualties to our guns which I attribute to the effective control of the personnel.

M. Morris Captain Commanding
88th Machine Gun Company

App. I (k)

RELIEFS AUGUST 1916 — 29th Divn.

Brigade / Unit	1	2	3	4	5	6	7	8	9	10	11	12	13	14	15	16	17	18	19	20	21	22	23	24	25	26	27	28	29	30	31	Relief Days
86th Brigade																																
2nd R. Fus.											L.S.R.	L.S.R.	L.S.R.	L.S.R.	L.S.R.	L.S.R.	L.S.R.	L.S.R.	L.S.R.													9/10, 19/20
1st Lanc's Fus.		Divisional Reserve																		R.S.R.	R.S.R.	R.S.R.	R.S.R.	R.S.R.	R.S.R.	R.S.R.	R.S.R.	R.S.R.				19/20, 29/30
16th Middlesex Regt.		Divisional Reserve																		R.S.L.	R.S.L.	R.S.L.	R.S.L.	R.S.L.	R.S.L.	R.S.L.	R.S.L.	R.S.L.				19/20, 29/30
1st R. Dub. Fus.											L.S.L.	L.S.L.	L.S.L.	L.S.L.	L.S.L.	L.S.L.	L.S.L.	L.S.L.	L.S.L.													9/10, 19/20
87th Brigade																																
1st KOSB.			L.S.L.	L.S.L.	L.S.L.	L.S.L.																L.S.R.	L.S.R.	L.S.R.	L.S.R.	L.S.R.						6/7, 26/27
2nd SW B.			L.S.R.	L.S.R.	L.S.R.	L.S.R.																L.S.L.	L.S.L.	L.S.L.	L.S.L.	L.S.L.						6/7, 26/27
1st R. Inniskillings			Divisional Reserve																													6/7, 9/10, 19/20, 26/27
1st Border Regt.			Divisional Reserve																													6/7, 9/10, 19/20, 26/27
88th Brigade																																
4th Worcester Regt.			R.S.R.	R.S.R.	R.S.R.	R.S.R.																							R.S.R.			9/10, 29/30
2nd Hants			R.S.L.	R.S.L.	R.S.L.	R.S.L.																							R.S.L.			9/10, 29/30
1st Essex												R.S.L.	R.S.L.	R.S.L.	R.S.L.	R.S.L.	R.S.L.	R.S.L.	R.S.L.													9/10, 19/20
Newfoundland Regt.												R.S.R.	R.S.R.	R.S.R.	R.S.R.	R.S.R.	R.S.R.	R.S.R.	R.S.R.													9/10, 19/20

— Reference —

- R.S.R. — Right Sector Right Sub-sector
- R.S.L. —   "   "   Left   "
- L.S.R. — Left   "   Right.   "
- L.S.L. —   "   "   Left.   "

REPORT ON THE ENEMY GAS ATTACK ON NIGHT OF

8/9th AUGUST 1916.

1. A gas attack by the enemy took place last night on the centre of the front held by this Division.
The total front affected by the gas discharge was from A 1. to A 7. but the gas appears to have been heaviest opposite the following two sections of the line.
A 1 - A 5.
A 7 - part of A 8.
held by the left Battalion of the Right Brigade, and left Company of the right Battalion of the Left Brigade respectively, among whom (especially the latter) the casualties were severe.

2. The gas alarm was sounded at 10.30 pm., when the gas cloud came rapidly over our trenches. It tavelled about 1000 yards in ten minutes. The men in some cases had not time to put on their helmets, although the alarm was taken up along the line immediately the presence of gas was detected, and gongs and Strombos Horns sounded.

3. The bombing and Lewis Gun post of the right Battalion (Right Brigade) on the railway, about I.11.b.67, reported that they heard a hissing sound to their left, though no gas actually passed over their lines.
The gas appears to have been emitted in two clouds, but the interval of time between the discharges cannot be ascertained.

4. The enemy bombarded the front trenches from A.5.a. to A 8. very heavily, and damaged the parapet in several places.
It seems probable that he intended to raid our trenches in this locality, but the heavy Lewis gun fire maintained by the garrison of these trenches on the German front line, together with enfilade machine gun fire from RAILWAY WOOD, and the artillery barrage, which was promptly applied, frustrated any such attempt, and the enemy did not leave his trenches.

5. The gas clouds were very dense for about half an hour, and hung about for a considerable time afterwards.
The clouds were very local in their effect, and travelled West by South as although the troops between H 15 - rs H 20 did not detect any gas, the troops and Battalion Headquarte in F 13 felt the effect. at
The Battalion Headquarters/POTIJZE hardly discerned the gas, but in YPRES behind the Ramparts, especially South of the MENIN Road, the cloud was very noticeable.

6. Helmets could be removed with safety at 12.30 am. and at 1.0 am, working parties and wiring parties in front of our trenches on the right of the Line resumed their work.

7. The gas travelled exceptionally far, as the cloud presumably from the 4th Division Area, reached Divisional Headquarters at A.25.d.1.4. a distance of nearly 13000 yards about 11.0 pm., and necessitated gas helmets being worn. This cloud was so local in its affect that the horse lines of the Headquarters and of the R.E. situated some 100 yards on either flank were not inconvenienced.

8. I append a list of the casualties from gassing reporte up to date. They were, I regret to say, severe due to the suddenness of the attack, and thenspeed at which the gas

App 1 (d)

SECRET.

29TH DIVISION CONFERENCE NO.10

held on 12th August, 1916.

Training of Machine Gun Companies.	1. The G.O.C. requested Brigadiers to pay greater attention to the discipline and training of the Machine Gun Companies in their Brigade Sectors. He had noticed that the gun teams were very slack and did not display the least keenness in their work. He wishes the attention of all Machine Gun Officers to be drawn to "Notes on the tactical employment of Machine Guns and Lewis Guns". All machine guns in position must fire at least 100 rounds on the German trenches every night.
Instruction of Officers in Trench Warfare.	2. Brigadiers must arrange to instruct the officers in their Brigades in Trench Warfare, both when in the line and in Reserve. All officers and senior N.C.Os. should be in possession of and study "Trench Orders".
Types of fire trenches to be adopted.	3. The G.O.C. wishes all fire trenches to be modelled in accordance with the attached diagrams A.1, A.2, in so far as this is feasible.
Organisation of work.	4. More satisfactory results will be obtained if greater attention is paid to the organisation of work. Battalion Pioneers should be used for revetting, maintenance of trench boards, etc.
Scheme of defence.	5. Copies of the general scheme of defence were handed to Brigadiers and C.R.E. (a copy was also sent to C.R.A.).
Protection against gas.	6. A great deal of practice is necessary in putting on gas helmets and in training men to wear their helmets for long periods. Special practice helmets are being issued for this purpose.
Training.	7. Brigadiers must consider the best method of training their Brigades in Reserve. Training programmes should be drawn up similar to that of the 86th Brigade.
Camps for 2nd Echelon.	8. The question of improvement of camps for the Second Echelon in view of the coming winter must be seriously considered. The necessity for construction of roads and horse standings was emphasised, vide diagrams B.1 and B.2 attached.

G. Fuller.
Lieut-Colonel, G.S.,
29th Division.

19th August, 1916.

App I (e)

Report on Gas Discharge on 29th Division Front
on night of 31st August/1st September.

1. A satisfactory gas discharge took place at 1.30 a.m. in the Right Sector of this Division front (from S.14 to No.4 Crater), the wind being S.W. and from 6 to 7 miles per hour. 83% of the 160 cylinders installed were discharged, the non-discharge of the remainder being due to defects in the apparatus etc.

2. It had been intended to discharge simultaneously 200 cylinders in the Left Sector on the front A.5.a. to A.7., but at the time detailed for the attack, the wind had not steadied down on this portion of the front and was veering between S. and S.W., so it was decided not to discharge the gas in this section.

3. According to the Battalion in the trenches from H.14 to Crater No.4, the enemy detected the gas from the hissing, and immediately sent up flares, followed almost at once by a red rocket bursting into white balls. The Germans also opened a heavy machine gun and rifle fire, directed principally against Craters 2 and 2.A, and along the Railway line. The enemy likewise retaliated with Trench Mortar bombs, which fell behind the firing line, and blew in the parapet in MUDDY LANE. Their artillery fire was however not heavy, and both their gun and Trench Mortar fire are reported as erratic.

4. Our artillery bombardment, which had been limited to the guns bearing on the Right Sector, opened at 1.40 a.m., and continued till 2.10 a.m. About 2 a.m. the enemy's rifle and machine gun fire dwindled and gradually ceased.

5. At 2.30 a.m., patrols went out towards I.12.a.0.4 and I.6.c.11.

The Newfoundland patrol on the right was unable to get through the hostile wire, but they heard the enemy coughing, running about on duck-boards, and flapping dugouts.

The Essex patrol reached the German wire, but could not penetrate it. The enemy were sending up flares from every second bay, and the patrol heard no noises in their trenches.

6. In the opinion of the Special Brigade Officer, the gas reached the Germans before they knew anything about it. The Patrols reported that there was a strong smell of gas on the ground.

7. There were no casualties among the Battalions in the Right Sector, but 2 men in a Trench Mortar Battery in this locality were wounded. The casualties in the Left Sector were also slight, 4 men of the Special Brigade being hit by shell fire.

App 2(a)

SECRET.

29TH DIVISION.

DISPOSITIONS - 2nd August, 1916.

RIGHT SECTOR. - 88th Infantry Brigade H.Q.

    Front Line. - 4th Worcester Regiment (Right)
                - 2nd Hampshire Regiment (Left)

    Support. - 1st Essex Regiment.

    Brigade Reserve. - Newfoundland Battalion.

LEFT SECTOR. - 87th Infantry Brigade H.Q.

    Front Line. - 2nd South Wales Borderers. (Right)
                - 1st K.O.S.Bs. (Left)

    Support. - 1st Border Regiment.

    Brigade Reserve. - 1st Royal Inniskilling Fusiliers.

DIVISIONAL RESERVE.

        86th Infantry Brigade.

        Headquarters .... WOOD A.30
        2nd Royal Fusiliers .... Camp "B"
        16th Middlesex Regt. .... Camp "C"
        1st Lancashire Fus. .... Camp "A"
        1st R. Dublin Fus. .... Camp "J"

2.8.16.

                                               Lieut-Colonel, G.S.,
                                               29th Division.

HEADQUARTERS. 29th DIVISION. INTELLIGENCE.
No. J.G.39
Date 5/5/16

App 2(b)

29TH DIVISION - LOCATION OF UNITS - 5-8-16.

86th Brigade.

Brigade Headquarters	Wood A.30 Camp C.
2nd Royal Fusiliers	Camp B.
1st Lancashire Fusiliers	Camp A.
16th Middlesex Regiment	Camp C.
1st Royal Dublin Fusiliers	Camp D.
86th Machine Gun Coy.	G.12.b.9.5.
86th Trench Mortar Battery	Camp C.

87th Brigade.

Brigade Headquarters	Ramparts YPRES (Left Sector).
2nd South Wales Borderers	Left Sub-sector Trenches.
1st Kings Own Scottish Borderers	Right Sub-sector Trenches.
1st Royal Inniskilling Fusiliers	Brigade Reserve.
1st Border Regiment.	Support.
Brigade Machine Gun Coy.	In the Trenches.
Trench Mortar Battery.	In the Trenches.

88th Brigade.

Brigade Headquarters	Ramparts YPRES (Right Sector).
4th Worcester Regiment	Right Sub-sector Trenches.
2nd Hampshire Regiment	Left Sub-sector Trenches.
1st Essex Regiment	Support.
Newfoundland Regiment	Brigade Reserve.
Brigade Machine Gun Coy.	In the Trenches.
Trench Mortar Battery.	In the Trenches.

5/8/16

App 2(c)

SECRET.

29TH DIVISION - LOCATION OF UNITS - 12TH AUGUST, 1916.

86th Brigade.

Brigade Headquarters	YPRES RAMPARTS, I.8.b.9.6.
2nd Royal Fusiliers	Right Sub-sector Trenches.
1st Royal Dublin Fusiliers	Left " "
1st Lancashire Fusiliers	Right Support.
16th Middlesex Regiment	Left "
86th Machine Gun Coy.	Trenches.
86th Trench Mortar Battery	"

87th Brigade.

Brigade Headquarters	A.30 Wood.
1st Border Regiment	Camp "A".
1st K.O.S.B.	" "B".
1st Royal Inniskilling Fusiliers	" "C".
2nd South Wales Borderers	" "D".
87th Machine Gun Coy.	G.12.b.9.5.
87th Trench Mortar Battery	Camp "C".

88th Brigade.

Brigade Headquarters	YPRES RAMPARTS, I.8.d.1.8.
Newfoundland Regiment	Right Sub-sector Trenches.
1st Essex Regiment	Left " "
4th Worcester Regiment	Right Support.
2nd Hampshire Regiment	Left "
88th Machine Gun Coy.	Trenches.
88th Trench Mortar Battery.	"

HEADQUARTERS.
29th DIVISION.
INTELLIGENCE.
No. G.39
Date. 12/8/16

Major, G.S.,
29th Division.

App 2(d) SECRET.

29th DIVISION - LOCATION OF UNITS - AT 9 A.M. 19th AUGUST 1916.

86th Brigade.

Brigade Headquarters	RAMPARTS YPRES I.8.a.95/70
1st Lancashire Fusiliers	Right Sub-sector Trenches.
16th Middlesex Regiment	Right Sector Left Sub-sector trenches.
2nd Royal Fusiliers	Left " Right " " "
1st Royal Dublin Fusiliers	Left " Left " " "
86th Machine Gun Coy.	Trenches
86th Trench Mortar Battery	"

87th Brigade.

Brigade Headquarters	"C" Camp
2nd South Wales Borderers	Canal Bank YPRES
1st. K.O.S.B.	Prison "
1st Border Regiment	"A" Camp
1st Royal Inniskilling Fusiliers	"C" "
87th Machine Gun Coy	Trenches
87th Trench Mortar Battery	"

88th Brigade.

Brigade Headquarters	RAMPARTS YPRES
1st Essex Regiment	"O" Camp
2nd Hampshire Regiment	YPRES
4th Worcester Regiment	YPRES
1st Newfoundland Regiment	"B" Camp
88th Machine Gun Coy	H.7.a.2.1
88th Trench Mortar Battery	G.6.a.8.8

Major, G.S.
29th Division.

App 2(c)

29TH DIVISION - LOCATION OF UNITS - 20TH AUGUST, 1916.

86th Brigade.

Brigade Headquarters	RAMPARTS YPRES I.8.a.95.70
1st Lancashire Fusiliers	Right Sector Right sub-sector trenches.
16th Middlesex Regiment	" " Left " "
2nd Royal Fusiliers	Right Support.
1st Royal Dublin Fusiliers	Left Support.
86th Machine Gun Company	Trenches.
86th Trench Mortar Battery	Trenches.

87th Brigade.

Brigade Headquarters	RAMPARTS YPRES I.8.a.95.70
1st K.O.S.Bs.	Left Sector Right sub-sector trenches.
2nd South Wales Borderers	" " Left " "
1st R. Inniskilling Fusiliers	Right Support.
1st Border Regiment	Left Support.
87th Machine Gun Company	Trenches.
87th Trench Mortar Battery	Trenches.

88th Brigade.

Brigade Headquarters	"C" Camp.
1st Essex Regiment	"O" "
2nd Hampshire Regiment	"C" "
4th Worcester Regiment	"A" "
1st Newfoundland Regiment	"B" "
88th Machine Gun Company	H.7.a.2.1
88th Trench Mortar Battery	G.6.a.8.8.

20.8.16.

Major, G.S.,
29th Division.

App 2(f)

SECRET.

29TH DIVISION - LOCATION OF UNITS - 26TH AUGUST, 1916.

86th Brigade.

Brigade Headquarters	RAMPARTS YPRES I.8.a.95.70.
1st Lancashire Fusiliers	Right Sector Right sub-sector trenches.
16th Middlesex Regiment	" " Left " "
2nd Royal Fusiliers	Right Support.
1st Royal Dublin Fusiliers	Left "
86th Machine Gun Coy.	Trenches.
86th Trench Mortar Battery	"

87th Brigade.

Brigade Headquarters	RAMPARTS YPRES I.8.a.95.70.
1st K.O.S.Bs.	Left Sector Right sub-sector trenches.
2nd South Wales Borderers	" " Left " "
1st R. Inniskilling Fusiliers	Right Support.
1st Border Regiment	Left "
87th Machine Gun Coy.	Trenches.
87th Trench Mortar Battery	"

88th Brigade.

Brigade Headquarters	"C" Camp.
1st Essex Regiment	"O" "
2nd Hampshire Regiment	"C" "
4th Worcester Regiment	"A" "
1st Newfoundland Regiment	"B" "
88th Machine Gun Coy.	H.7.a.2.1.
88th Trench Mortar Battery	G.6.a.8.8.

26.8.16.

Major, G.S.,
29th Division.

App 2(7)

SECRET.

29TH DIVISION - LOCATION OF UNITS - 31ST AUGUST, 1916.

86th Brigade.

Brigade Headquarters.	Camp C.
2nd Royal Fusiliers.	" B.
1st Lancashire Fusiliers.	" A.
16th Middlesex Regiment.	" C.
1st Royal Dublin Fusiliers.	" O.
86th Machine Gun Company.	" H.7.a.2.1.
86th Trench Mortar Battery.	" A.30.d.

87th Brigade.

Brigade Headquarters.	RAMPARTS, YPRES, I.8.a.95.70.
1st K.O.S.B.	Left Sector, Right sub-sector trenches.
2nd South Wales Borderers.	" " Left " "
1st Royal Inniskilling Fusiliers.	Right Support.
1st Border Regiment.	Left "
87th Machine Gun Company.	Trenches.
87th Trench Mortar Battery.	"

88th Brigade.

Brigade Headquarters.	RAMPARTS, YPRES, I.8.d.10.65.
1st Newfoundland Regiment.	Right Sector, Right sub-sector trenches.
1st Essex Regiment.	" " Left " "
4th Worcester Regiment.	Right Support.
2nd Hampshire Regiment.	Left "
88th Machine Gun Coy.	Trenches.
88th Trench Mortar Battery.	"

31st August, 1916.

Major, G.S.,
29th Division.

App. 3(a)

SECRET.   Copy No. 3

29TH DIVISION OPERATION ORDER NO.53.

8th August, 1916.

1. The 86th Brigade will relieve the 87th Brigade in the Left Sector of the line on the nights 8th/9th and 9th/10th August. Moves and reliefs will be carried out as in the attached schedule.

2. Details will be arranged direct between Brigades concerned.

3. (a) The two Battalions 86th Brigade that go up on the night of 8th/9th August will on arrival in YPRES come under command of the G.O.C. 87th Brigade as Brigade Reserve, Left Sector.
   (b) The two Battalions 87th Brigade that come out of YPRES on the night 8th/9th August will come under command of the G.O.C. 86th Brigade as part of the Divisional Reserve.

4. The 87th Machine Gun Company and Trench Mortar Battery will be relieved by the corresponding units of the 86th Brigade on the night 8th/9th August but a proportion of the detachments of the 87th Brigade Machine Guns and Trench Mortars will remain in the line until the night of the 9th/10th to assist the incoming units.

5. The G.O.C. 86th Brigade will take over command of the Left Sector of the line on completion of the relief on the night of 9th/10th August.

6. Time table of train service will be issued later.

7. Completion of all moves and reliefs will be reported to these Headquarters. The new dispositions will be forwarded to these Headquarters by 9 a.m. on the 10th.

8. The 87th Brigade Signal Section in the line will not be relieved.

9. Acknowledge by wire.

D. Ovey Major.

for Lieut-Colonel, G.S.,
                29th Division.

Issued at 2.15 p.m.

Copies 1 - 5   General Staff.   11   Officer i/c Sigs.
         6   86th Brigade.   12   1/2nd Monmouth Regt.
         7   87th Brigade.   13 - 17 A.A. & Q.M.G.
         8   88th Brigade.   18   VIIIth Corps.
         9   C.R.A. 20th Divl. Arty.   19   4th Division.
        10   C.R.E.   20   3rd Canadian Divn.

Date.	Unit.	From.	To.	Remarks.
Night of 8th/9th August.	2 Battalions 86th Brigade.	Camps A.B.C.O.	YPRES.	Train.
	86th Machine Gun Coy.	H.7.A.	Trenches.	March.
	86th Trench Mortar Battery.	A.30.D.	Trenches.	March.
	2 Battalions 87th Brigade.	YPRES.	Camps A.B.C.O.	Train. Come into Divisional Reserve.
	87th Machine Gun Coy.	Trenches.	H.7.A.	March.
	87th Trench Mortar Battery.	Trenches.	A.30.D.	March.
Night of 9th/10th August.	2 Battalions 86th Brigade.	YPRES.	Trenches.	March.
	2 Battalions 87th Brigade.	Trenches.	Camps A.B.C.O.	Train from Asylum, YPRES. Come into Divisional Reserve.
	Headquarters 87th Brigade.	YPRES.	Camp C.	
	Headquarters 86th Brigade and 2 Battalions.	Camps A.B.C.O.	YPRES.	Train.

App 3(4)

S E C R E T. Copy No. 3

29TH DIVISION OPERATION ORDER NO.54.

August 18th, 1916.

1. The 87th Brigade will relieve the 86th Brigade in the Left Sector of the line, and the 86th Brigade on relief from the Left Sector will take over the Right Sector from the 88th Brigade, on the nights of the 18th/19th and 19/20th August, in accordance with the attached Moves Table.

2. The 88th Brigade on relief will be in Divisional Reserve.

3. Details of moves will be arranged direct between Brigades concerned.

4. (a) The two battalions 86th Brigade that move from YPRES to the trenches Right Sector on the night of the 18th/19th, will on arrival come under the command of the G.O.C., 88th Brigade.
   (b) The two battalions 87th Brigade that move up to YPRES on the night of the 18th/19th August will on arrival come under the command of the G.O.C., 86th Brigade, as Brigade Reserve, Left Sector.
   (c) The two battalions 88th Brigade that move from YPRES to Camp C on the night of the 18th/19th August, will on arrival come under the command of the G.O.C., 87th Brigade, as Divisional Reserve.

5. The 88th and 86th Machine Gun Companies and Trench Mortar Batteries will be relieved by the corresponding units of the 86th and 87th Brigades respectively on the night of the 18th/19th August, but a proportion of the detachments of the 88th and 86th Machine Guns and Trench Mortars will remain in the line until the night of the 19th/20th August, to assist the incoming units. The relief by the 87th Machine Guns and Trench Mortars will be completed by 11 p.m. on the 18th August.

6. The G.Os.C. 86th and 87th Brigades, will take over the commands of the Right and Left Sectors respectively on completion of the reliefs on the night of the 19th/20th August.

7. The time-table of the train service will be issued later by the A.A. & Q.M.G.

8. The Brigade Signal Sections in the line will not be relieved.

9. Completion of all moves and reliefs will be reported to these Headquarters. The new dispositions will be forwarded to these Headquarters by 9 a.m. on the 19th and 20th instant.

10. Acknowledge by wire.

C.G. Fuller.
Lieut-Colonel, G.S.,
29th Division.

Issued at ...11.0 am
Copies 1 - 5 General Staff.   11 Off. i/c Sigs.
       6 86th Brigade.   12 O.C. 1/2nd Monmouth Regiment.
       7 87th Brigade.   13 - 17 A.A. & Q.M.G.
       8 88th Brigade.   18 VIIIth Corps.
       9 C.R.A. 20th Divl. Arty.   19 4th Division.
      10 C.R.E.   20 3rd Canadian Divn.

TABLE OF MOVES.

Date.	Unit.	From.	To.	Remarks.
Night of 18th/19th August.	2 Battalions 87th Bde.	Camps A.B.C.O.	YPRES, Left Sector.	Train.
	87th Machine Gun Coy.	H.7.a.	Trenches, Left Sector.	March.
	87th Trench Mortar Batty.	A.30.d.	Trenches, Left Sector.	March.
	2 Battalions 86th Bde.	YPRES, Left Sector.	Trenches, Right Sector.	March.
	86th Machine Gun Coy.	Trenches, Left Sector.	Trenches, Right Sector.	March.
	86th Trench Mortar Batty.	Trenches, Left Sector.	Trenches, Right Sector.	March.
	2 Battalions 88th Bde.	Trenches, Right Sector.	Camps A.B.C.O.	Train.
	88th Machine Gun Coy.	Trenches, Right Sector.	H.7.a.	March.
	88th Trench Mortar Batty.	Trenches, Right Sector.	A.30.d.	March.
Night of 19th/20th August.	Headquarters, 87th Bde.	Camp C.	YPRES, Left Sector.	Train.
	2 Battalions, 87th Bde.	Camps A.B.C.O.	YPRES, Left Sector.	Train.
	2 Battalions, 87th Bde.	YPRES, Left Sector.	Trenches, Left Sector.	March.
	Headquarters, 83th Bde.	YPRES, Left Sector.	YPRES, Right Sector.	March.
	2 Battalions, 86th Bde. Trenches.	YPRES, Left Sector.	YPRES, Right Sector.	March.
	Headquarters, 88th Bde.	YPRES, Right Sector.	Camp C.	Train.
	2 Battalions, 88th Bde.	YPRES, Right Sector.	Camp A.B.C.O.	Train.

App 3(c)

SECRET.   Copy No..... 4 .....

29TH DIVISION ORDER NO. 55.

25th August, 1916.

1.   A total of 360 Gas Cylinders will be installed in the front line on the nights of the 27th/28th and 28th/29th August as follows :— *(27/28 and 64 cylinders on night 28/29th)*
   96 ~~80~~ cylinders ~~per~~ night in the Right Sector between
       Trench H.14 and No.4 Crater.
   100 cylinders per night in the Left Sector between
       Trenches A.5.a and A.7.

2.   The 86th and 87th Brigades will detail carrying parties as shewn in the attached Appendix.
   (a) The 86th Brigade parties will report at point I.9.d.8.4 on the MENIN ROAD on each of the above nights.
       Cylinders will be carried up to the front line via MENIN ROAD - RAILWAY - WEST LANE and DUCK WALK, and the returning carriers will follow the route MUD LANE - F.6 - RAILWAY FARM - RAILWAY track - MENIN ROAD.
   (b) The 87th Brigade parties will report at POTIJZE at point I.4.c.2.9 on each of the above nights.
       Cylinders will be carried up to the front line via HAYMARKET and DUKE STREET, and carriers will return via FLEET STREET and STRAND.

3.   16 cylinders each weighing 150 lbs. will be installed in each bay in the Right Sector, and 20 cylinders in each bay in the Left Sector. Four men will be detailed to each cylinder, two men carrying and two in relief.

4.   Each cylinder is provided with a pole. On completion of work, poles will be dumped at the East end of the square in YPRES (I.8.c.6.9½).

5.   Carrying parties and officers in charge should as far as possible be the same on each night. Parties should be sized and numbered before arrival at the dumps. Each party to carry 1 pick and 2 shovels, and each man to be provided with a sandbag to act as a shoulder pad.

6.   The 86th and 87th Brigades will each detail an officer to supervise the offloading of the lorries at their dumps on the MENIN ROAD, and at POTIJZE respectively. These officers will each be assisted by an N.C.O., detailed from the Special Brigade R.E.

7.   Guides will be told off by the Special Brigade R.E. to meet each party at the dumps, and to conduct them to the emplacements.

8.   All other traffic in the trenches up which the cylinders are being carried, will stop while the carrying is in progress. Wounded men even will not be moved, but will be attended to on the spot, and medical arrangements will be made accordingly.

9.   All men handling stores, and all those in the vicinity of where cylinders are being or have been installed, will carry P.H.G. Helmets in the Alert position.

                                                  / Vermorel

- 2 -

Vermorel Sprayers will be ready for spraying the trenches in the event of any damage being done to the cylinders by either shell or bullets.

10. Smoking will on no account be permitted.

11. It is important that silence be maintained.

12. All reference to these arrangements on the telephone is prohibited.

13. "L" Coy. Special Brigade, will detail one sapper to attend to each group of 6 bays, as soon as the cylinders are in place. Troops in the trenches will assist them in any repairs to bays that may be required. Troops of the Special Brigade can be distinguished after dark by the red, green and white brassards, which they wear on the right arm.

14. Brigades will arrange to have 30 filled sandbags ready near each bay in which cylinders are being placed, to assist the Special Brigade personnel in building in the emplacements, after the cylinders have been placed in position.

15. Conferences of the Officers detailed to supervise carrying parties will be held on 26th instant at 3 p.m. at the respective Brigade Headquarters. 2nd/Lieut. JONES and Lieut. WALTERS of the Special Brigade R.E. will attend these Conferences, at 86th and 87th Brigade Headquarters respectively, and will explain the detailed arrangements to the Officers concerned.

16. Acknowledge by wire.

CF Fuller.
Lieut-Colonel, G.S.,
29th Division.

Issued at 11. 0 p.m.

Copies 1 - 5 General Staff.   12   O.C. 1/2nd Monmouth Regt.
       6   86th Brigade.   13 - 17   A.A. & Q.M.G.
       7   87th Brigade.   18 - 20   O.C. "L" Coy. Spec. Bde.R.E.
       8   88th Brigade.   21   VIIIth Corps.
       9   C.R.A.   22   4th Division.
      10   C.R.E.   23   38th Division.
      11   Officer i/c Sigs.   24   Divisional Gas Officer.

APPENDIX.

86th Brigade.

Dump.	Date.	Party No.	Strength.	Time of arrival at Dump.
I.9.d.8.4. MENIN DUMP.	27th	1	64	10.0 p.m.
		2	64	10.10 p.m.
		3	64	10.40 p.m.
		4	64	10.50 p.m.
		5	64	11.20 p.m.
		6	64	11.30 p.m.
	28th	1	64	10.0 p.m.
		2	64	10.10 p.m.
		3	64	10.40 p.m.
		4	64	10.50 p.m.

87th Brigade.

Dump.	Date.	Party No.	Strength.	Time of arrival at Dump.
I.4.c.2.9. POTIJZE DUMP.	27th	1	80	10.0 p.m.
		2	80	10.15 p.m.
		3	80	10.40 p.m.
		4	80	10.55 p.m.
		5	80	11.20 p.m.
	28th	1	80	10.10 p.m.
		2	80	10.15 p.m.
		3	80	10.40 p.m.
		4	80	10.55 p.m.
		5	80	11.20 p.m.

Each party will have in addition to the above 1 Officer and 4 N.C.Os. to supervise the work.

SECRET.

86th Brigade.
87th Brigade.
88th Brigade.
C.R.A.
C.R.E.
Officer i/c Signals.
O.C. 1/2nd Monmouth Regiment.
A.A. & Q.M.G.
O.C. "L" Coy. Spec. Bde. R.E.
VIIIth Corps.
4th Division.
38th Division.
Divisional Gas Officer.

CORRECTION TO 29TH DIVISION ORDER NO.55.

Paragraph 1.   Delete lines 4 and 5, and substitute the following :-

"96 cylinders on the night of 27th/28th instant and 64 cylinders on the night of the 28th/29th instant in the Right Sector between Trench H.14. and No. 4. Crater."

C.J. Fuller.

Lieut-Colonel, G.S.,
29th Division.

26th August, 1916.

App 3(d)

SECRET. Copy No. 3.

29TH DIVISION ORDER NO. 56.

August 27th, 1916.

1. The 88th Brigade will relieve the 86th Brigade in the Right Sector on the 29th and 30th August in accordance with the attached "Moves Table".

2. On relief the 86th Brigade will be in Corps Reserve.

3. Details of moves will be arranged direct between Brigades concerned.

4. The 88th Machine Gun Coy. AND 88th Trench Mortar Battery will relieve the 86th Machine Gun Coy. and 86th Trench Mortar Battery on the 28th instant, the latter leaving a proportion of their detachments in the line until the night of the 29th/30th to assist the incoming unit

5.(a) The 88th Machine Gun Coy., the 88th Trench Mortar Battery, and the two Battalions of 88th Brigade that move to YPRES on the 28th and 29th August will come under the command of the G.O.C., 86th Brigade, one Battalion to form the Brigade Reserve and one Battalion and 1 Section 88th Machine Gun Coy. to form Divisional Reserve, the name of the latter Battalion to be notified to Divisional Headquarters.
 (b) The two Battalions of the 86th Brigade that move from YPRES to Camps A.B.C.O. on the night of the 29th August will on arrival come under the command of the G.O.C., 88th Brigade, as Corps Reserve.

6. The relief of the two Battalions 86th Brigade in the front line by the two Battalions 88th Brigade from YPRES on the 30th August will be carried out as far as possible during the day. In view of possible operations, it is important that the relief should be completed as soon after dark as feasible.

7. The G.O.C. 88th Brigade will take over command of the Right Sector on completion of relief on the 30th instant. He will notify Divisional Headquarters which Battalion has been allocated as Divisional Reserve.

8. The time table of train services will be issued later by the A.A. & Q.M.G.

9. The Brigade Signal Section in the line will not be relieved.

10. Completion of moves and reliefs will be reported to these Headquarters. The new dispositions will be forwarded to these Headquarters by 9 a.m. on 31st instant.

11. Acknowledge by wire.

C.G. Fuller
Lieut-Colonel, G.S.,
29th Division.

Issued at 3 p.m.

Copies 1 - 5 General Staff. 11 Officer i/c Signals.
       6   86th Brigade.   12 1/2nd Monmouth Regiment.
       7   87th Brigade.   13 - 17 A.A. & Q.M.G.
       8   88th Brigade.   18 VIIIth Corps.
       9   C.R.A.   19 4th Division.
      10   C.R.E.   20 38th Division.

MOVES TABLE.

Date.	Unit.	From.	To.	Remarks.
Night of 28/29th August.	88th M. Gun Coy.	H.7.a.	Trenches.	March.
	88th T. M. Batty.	A.30.d.	"	"
	86th M. Gun Coy.	Trenches.	H.7.a.	"
	86th T. M. Batty.	"	A.30.d.	"
Night of 29th/30th August.	2 Bns. 88th Bde.	Camps A.B.C.O.	YPRES (Right Sector)	Train.
	2 Bns. 86th Bde.	YPRES (Right Sector)	Camps A.B.C.O.	"
Night of 30th/31st August.	2 Bns. 88th Bde.	YPRES (Right Sector)	Trenches.	March.
	H.Q. 88th Bde.	Camp C.	YPRES (Right Sector)	Train.
	2 Bns. 88th Bde.	Camps A.B.C.O.	YPRES (Right Sector)	"
	H.Q. 86th Bde.	YPRES (Right Sector)	Camp C.	"
	2 Bns. 86th Bde.	Trenches.	Camps A.B.C.O.	"

App 3(e)

S E C R E T.   Copy No. 5.

29TH DIVISION ORDER NO. 57.

28th August, 1916.

1. If the wind is favourable a gas attack on the enemy's line will take place on the night of the 29th/30th August, at 1.30 a.m. (denoted by Zero in these Orders), in accordance with the following programme :-

   Zero - Gas discharge commences.
   0.10 - Bombardment by Heavy and Divisional Artillery commences. Machine Guns fire bursts of rapid fire.
   0.20 - Gas discharge ceases.
   0.40 - Bombardment by artillery ends and Machine Guns cease fire.
   1.00 - Patrols move out.

2. The gas will be discharged as rapidly as possible from the whole of the cylinders installed on the Division Front. All cylinders will be closed at 0.20.

3. The artillery bombardment will be carried out in accordance with the programme arranged by the C.R.A. The Artillery will not open fire till 0.10.

4. The 86th and 87th Brigades will arrange for Machine gun fire to be opened at 0.10 on the enemy's main support and communication trenches, and to continue in bursts of rapid fire until 0.40.

5. Patrols will be sent out at 1.00 by the 86th and 87th Brigades towards points I.12.a.0.4 and I.5.b.45.75 respectively, in order to ascertain the effects of the gas attack. Each of these patrols will be accompanied by 2 men of the Special Brigade. These men will report at 7 p.m. on the 29th instant at 86th and 87th Brigade Headquarters respectively.

6. The decision as to whether the wind is favourable will be telephoned to Captain J. A. CARPENTER, Special Brigade, at 86th Brigade Headquarters shortly after 10 p.m. on the 29th instant.
   The ultimate decision as to whether the wind is favourable for the discharge will rest with 2/Lieut. JONES and Lieut. WALTERS in the Right and Left Sectors respectively, who will telephone their decisions to Battalion Headquarters for transmission to Artillery Group Commanders, Brigade and Divisional Headquarters.

7. The following code will be used in the above messages :-
   If the wind is favourable - YES.
   If the wind is unfavourable - NO.

8. No information or instructions regarding these operations are to be sent over the telephone, or over the wires, except in code.

9. All troops in the front line system on the night of the 29th/30th instant will wear their gas helmets in the "ALERT" position.

10. Watches will be synchronised by the General Staff at 7 p.m. on the 29th instant.

11. Acknowledge by wire.

                                                            J. Fuller

                                                 Lieut-Colonel, G.S.,

                                                       29th Division.

Issued at *11.30 p.m.*

```
Copies  1 - 5  General Staff.          12      O.C. 1/2nd Monmouth Regt.
        6      86th Brigade.      13 - 17      A.A. & Q.M.G.
        7      87th Brigade.      18 - 20      "J" Coy. Spec. Bde. R.E.
        8      88th Brigade.          21       VIIIth Corps.
        9      C.R.A.                 22       4th Division.
       10      C.R.E.                 23       38th Division.
       11      Officer i/c Signals.   24       Divisional Gas Officer.
                                      25.      VIIIth Corps Heavy
                                                          Artillery.
```

SECRET

AMENDMENT TO 29th DIVISION ORDER NO. 57.
----

1. With reference to 29th Division Order No. 57 of the 28th August, paragraph 7, the following code will be employed in the forthcoming operations, in lieu of that laid down in the paragraph abovementioned.

    (a). Wind is favourable for discharge of gas   - BERLIN

    (b). Wind is not favourable for discharge of gas.   - HANOVER.

    (c). Is wind favourable for discharge of gas   - COLOGNE.

    (d). Discharge gas at _____   - DRESDEN.

    (e). It is possible that gas will be discharged to-night   - FRANKFORT.

2. Message No. 438 in the Code Book will not be used until code words for the direction of the wind have been issued.

3. Acknowledge by wire.

G. Fuller.

Lieut. Colonel, G.S,

29th Division.

29th August 1916.

App 3(b)

SECRET.　　　　　　　　　　　　　　　　　　Copy No. 3

29th DIVISION ORDER NO. 58.

30th August 1916.

1.　　With reference to 29th Division Order No. 57, the gas attack will be carried out to-night 30/31st August, if the wind is favourable, or on the first favourable night subsequent to this date.

2.　　The arrangements for notifying whether the wind is favourable, and for the gas attack will be the same as those laid down in the Division Order above quoted except that the 88th Brigade will carry out the duties allotted therein to the 86th Brigade. Captain Carpenter will be at 88th Brigade Headquarters instead of at 86th Brigade Headquarters (vide para 6 of Order No.57).

3.　　The relief of the 86th Brigade by the 88th Brigade ordered in Division Order No.56 will be completed by 12 midnight to-night.

4.　　The 88th Brigade will send out a patrol towards point I.6.c.11., in addition to the patrol towards point I.12.a.0.4.,(vide para 5 of Division Order No.57.).

5.　　Until the attack has taken place, watches will be synchronised by the General Staff at 7.p.m. every evening.

6.　　Acknowledge by wire.

C.F. Fuller.

Lieut Colonel, G.S.
29th Division.

Issued at.. 11.30 A.M.

Copies 1 - 5 General Staff.　　　　12 O.C.1/2nd Monmouth Regt.
　　　　 6 86th Brigade.　　　　　　13 - 17 A.A. & Q.M.G.
　　　　 7 87th Brigade.　　　　　　18 - 20 "J" Coy. Spec. Bde. R.E.
　　　　 8 88th Brigade.　　　　　　21 VIIIth Corps.
　　　　 9 C.R.A.　　　　　　　　　 22 4th Division.
　　　　10.C.R.E.　　　　　　　　　 23 38th Division.
　　　　11 Off. i/c Signals.　　　　24 Divisional Gas Officer.
　　　　　　　　　　　　　　　　　　25 VIIIth Corps Heavy Artillery.

Headquarters,

VIIIth Corps.

app 4.

WORK REPORT - 29TH DIVISION.

28th, 29th, 30th August, 1916.

RIGHT SECTOR.

- **Firing Line.** Revetting and General repair. Wire improved.
- **H.21.** Alternative position for Machine Gun completed.
- **H.20.** Wiring New Trench continued.
- **S.23.** Wire strengthened, drainage improved.
- **F.11.** Wiring completed in front of New Trench.
- **A.1, A.3, A.5.** Generally repaired and maintained.
- **DUCK WALK Trench.** Revetting done under R.E. supervision.
- **MUDDY LANE.** Trench drained. Wire strengthened in front of 1.A Crater.
- **S.21.** New Gun pit built for Light T.M. Battery.
- **HAYMARKET and WEST LANE.** Generally repaired and maintained.
- **PICCADILLY.** Work continued. Another 50 yards dug ready to receive "U" Frames. 150 yards have been framed, revetted and floored, and 150 yards parapet revetted.
- **DRAIN.** Work commenced on a drain from Front line, North of CRUMP FARM to CAMBRIDGE ROAD.
- **Elephant Shelters.** Work continued in covering with shock and bursting courses on erected elephants at WHITE CHATEAU, HUSSAR and DRAGOON FARMS.
- **ECOLE.** Protection continued on strong point Cellars Nos. 46, 43, 44, 22 - 25.
  No.27 nearly completed including latrine and cookhouse.
- **WHITE CHATEAU Cellar.** Protection and Tunnelling between 2 Machine Gun emplacements continued.
- **RED CHATEAU Cellar 30.** Protection of both large and small cellars continued.
- **Signal Test Dugout.** Framing completed, concreting floor.
- **YPRES.** Bridge demolition preparations. LILLE GATE - water diverted and work continued. POPERINGHE GATE - store protected, powder stored. WOODEN SALLY PORTS - Complete except obstacles.

- 2 -

LEFT SECTOR.

Firing Line. Repairing parados and parapets. Trench boards repaired and relaid. Borrow trenches dug. Wire strengthened. Parts deepened to 4 ft. and revetted.

X.5. New drain dug. Trench boards relaid.

X.8. New drain dug.

B.10.a. 240 yards of trench deepened.

FLEET STREET. 8 "U" Frames fixed in trench and a good deal of sandbag revetment done.

GARDEN STREET. Trench deepened and widened in parts and revetted.

CONGREVE WALK. Drains dug and enlarged, also a certain amount of revetment done.

STRAND. Trench boards repaired and relaid. Revetment repaired. Camouflage built.

BIRCH WALK. Drainage improved, trench boards repaired and relaid.

NEW JOHN STREET. Trench deepened.

Elephant Shelters. Work continued in covering with shock and bursting courses on erected elephants in ST. JEAN, VINERY and LANCER FARM.

CANAL Bridges. Preparing for demolition. Fixing cleats for exposure boards. Repairing handrails and replacing chesses.

Divisional Baths. Screens completed for outside passage and roof of same.

ST. JEAN. Cellars and dugouts. No.1 - strutting completed and passage to Machine Gun emplacements.
No.13. Large elephant erected.
No.12. 1½ small elephants and passage to cellar.
No.17. Roof strutted.
No.7. Cellar strutted.
No.11. 1 large elephant.

ST. JEAN ROAD. Railway repaired between Cross Roads and Barrier.

PROWSE FARM. Machine Gun emplacement, floor concreted, shuttering erected.

Drainage. 100 yards BELLEWAARDEBEEK cleared. 300 yards drain for WEST LANE cleared, and 200 yards for ST. JEAN cleared.

31st August, 1916.

Major-General,
Commanding 29th Division.

Headquarters,

VIIIth Corps.

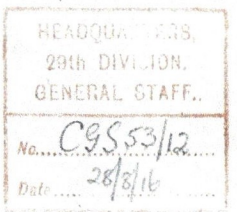
HEADQUARTERS,
29th DIVISION.
GENERAL STAFF.
No. CGS 53/12
Date 28/8/16

WORK REPORT - 29TH DIVISION.

RIGHT SECTOR.

Firing Line. Generally repaired and improved. Extra sumps dug, trench boards repaired or replaced where necessary, wire considerably strengthened.

MUDDY LANE. Drained and repaired. Generally cleaned up. Wiring improved.

F.5. Drained and repaired. Head cover added.

S.21. Cleaned and drained. Wire entanglements improved.

DUCK WALK. Drained and improved.

WEST LANE. Generally repaired and drained.

HAYMARKET. Drain dug. Generally cleaned and repaired. Sides of trench revetted with iron. Trench boards relaid.

PICCADILLY. Work continued, trench widened and deepened. Frames fixed in, and more trench boards laid. Revetted with iron. Drained.

X.1 and X.2. Generally repaired.

ECOLE Strong Point. No.46 cellar - new entrance and traversing completed. Protection continued.
Nos. 22 - 25 cellars - Protection continued.
No. 27 cellar - Protection nearly completed.
No. 29 cellar - Protection continued for first shelter and clearing commenced for second.

WHITE CHATEAU. - M.G. position - No.32 elephant strutted, protection commenced. Tunnelling between two positions commenced.

RED CHATEAU. - M.G. positions - No.30 protection of large elephant continued. Small elephant erected and strutted.
No. 51 - Clearing for elephant completed. Front protecting wall built, ground frame fixed.
Signal dugout No.53 - Work continued.

MENIN ROAD - Drying Room - Concreting floor and ceiling.
Screening Roads - Continued.
Notice boards - Continued.

HORNWORK. Gas curtains continued.

YPRES. - Bridges, revising demolition scheme. MENIN GATE completed. LILLE GATE in hand. POPERINGHE ROAD new arrangements for storage of explosives made. Wooden Sally Port Bridges nearly complete. Lock Gates cleared and thrown down.

HUSSAR FARM. 1 - 6 section elephant, earth course 2nd roof completed. 1 - 4 section elephant strutted. Floor concreted. End wall concrete built. 2nd roof built.
Cellar bursting course put on.

DRAGOON FARM. 1 - 6 section elephant. End Wall commenced.
1 - 6 section elephant concrete floor completed.

RIGHT BRIGADE H.Q. Ventilating completed. Great improvement.

LEFT SECTOR.

Firing Line. A great deal of work has been necessary in repairing, especially the left sub-sector, owing to retaliation by the enemy. Parapets and parados repaired and revetted. Ammunition recesses constructed and improved. Trenches drained and trench boards relaid. Wire entanglements improved.

S.8. Deepened and revetted. Fire position improved. Drain dug. Parados built up.

NEW JOHN STREET and S.10.A. Trench cleared and revetted. Fire positions improved. Damage repaired.

MONMOUTH TRENCH. Considerable progress. "U" Frames fixed. Breast work thickened. Revetted.

FLEET STREET and STRAND. Parapet heightened, trench boards fixed. Revetted where necessary, new frames added. Drained, improved and deepened.

POTIJZE CHATEAU and CONGREVE WALK. Drains marked out and dug. Borrow drain deepened. Floor boards repaired and relaid. Revetted where necessary.

GARDEN STREET. Generally repaired and revetted. Drain cleared and widened in parts.

LA BRIQUE POST. Borrow pit dug. Breast work strengthened. Trench drained.

CANAL BANK. Work on new Cookhouse nearly completed.

MILL COTTAGES, - T.M. Emplacement - Concreting 3 sides of pit completed. 8' of ammunition gallery made.

POTIJZE CHATEAU. 1 - 5 section elephant, windows bricked up.
1 - 5 section elephant, earth course over elephant.
1 - 4 section elephant erected. Partly concreted, end framed.
Cellar - concreting floor completed. Foundation wall cut through for cables.

VINERY. 1 side and 1 end of shell proof cover concreted.

LANCER FARM. 1 - 6 section elephant, roof completed and strutted. Floor concreted.
1 - 4 section elephant side and end concreted, strutting commenced

ST. JEAN ROAD. Fixing screens continued.
Repairs to Railway finished between ST. JEAN and WIELTJE.

ST. JEAN - Cellar and dugouts - No.12 finished, elephant erected in Nos. 11 and 13.
Drainage - BELLEWAARDEBEEK cleared from past PICCADILLY drain to WEST LANE. Cleared to CONGREVE WALK.

PROWSE FARM. Machine Gun emplacement - floor concreted.

28th August, 1916.

Major-General,
Commanding 29th Division.

Headquarters,
VIIIth Corps.

WORK REPORT - 29th DIVISION.

RIGHT SECTOR.

FIRING LINE.   General repairs, resetting trench boards, making Sump and repairing wire.

Sectors 1 and 1a.   Trenches connecting the two trenches repaired.

Gully Trench.   Trench widened from 3' to 4'6".

Duke Street.   Building gun-pit for T.M. Draining and resetting trench boards.

Haymarket.   Preparing gun-pit for T.M. Draining.

Duck Walk.   Broadened communication trench from Duck Walk ~~separate line~~ and fitting in "U" frames.

Cambridge Road.   Drainage ditch running along side Cambridge Road into a communication trench.

X Line.   X 3 deepening and widening trench, cleaning and resetting trench boards.

LEFT SECTOR.

FIRING LINE.   A 6 to A 10.   Drains cut and deepened.   Parapet and parados prepared where blown in.

B 9 to B 12.   Damage repaired, trenches cleaned and drained. Parapet and parados thickened and revetted.

Fleet Street.   Parapet raised.

Strand.   Damage repaired, 65 trench boards laid.

Monmouth Trench.   68 yards of breast work built to 4'6" high and 8' broad at top and 15 feet at bottom.

Garden Street.   Deepened for 60 yards and 30 "U" frames put in.

Durham Trench.   Parapet improved.

Prowse Farm.   Preparing ground for ~~several~~ concret M. G. emplacements.

Garden of Eden.   30 yards widened and deepened, parapet heightened.

CONGREVE WALK.   Drained.

X LINE.   Trench cleared and drained.

Shell Proof Covers.   POTIJZE CHATEAU.   One six section elephant completed.   One six section elephant half completed.

VINERY.   One six section elephant erected.

- 2 -

LANCER FARM. One six section elephant and one four section elephant being constructed.

HUSSAR FARM. One six section elephant and one four section elephant concreting commenced.

DRAGOON FARM. Two six section elephants nearly completed, also one cellar.

ECOLE Strong Post. Cellar No.46 sandbagged, protection proceeded with. New entrance in hand.

HEADMASTER'S HOUSE. Work nearly completed.

Cellars Nos. 22, 25 and 27. Work/Very nearly completed.

No. 32 WHITE CHATEAU. Elephant erected, loophole box for Machine Gun emplacement fixed. Sandbag protection commenced.

No. 30 RED CHATEAU. Elephant erected.

CANAL. Bridge A.1 and AUCTION Bridge preparing for demolition.

DRAINS. Cleaning out drains. BELLEWAARDEBEEK cleared 500 yards. HAYMARKET drained 400 yards. Draining cross line from North of BELLEWAARDEBEEK 250 yards.

Road near POPERINGHE. Work is being done on the track from G.4.c.7.4 to A.25.b.2.1.

Cable Trench near WHITE CHATEAU. Length of trench dug 647 yards. Cable laid and trench filled in 245 yards. Total cable to date 2070 yards.

24th August, 1916.

Major-General,
Commanding 29th Division.

Headquarters,

VIIIth Corps.

HEADQUARTERS,
29th DIVISION,
GENERAL STAFF.
No. C.G.S. 53/12
Date 17.8.16

WORK REPORT.

Right Sector.

Firing Line.
From A.1 to DUKE STREET 50 sump holes dug and trench boards relaid.
One bay and parapet to left of A.1 and 3 traverses and one bay
to the right of A.3, thickened and revetted.
Trench leading into Gully and drain and Gully deepened.
No. 1 Sap entrance: parapet raised and thickened 67 yards.
H.19 deepened and parapet repaired.
S.21 thickened and widened.

GULLY Trench. Revetted and deepened 30 yards, and drain for 300 yards (drain 2ft. by 2 ft.)

Ditch between junction of GULLY and CAMBRIDGE ROAD and junction of CAMBRIDGE ROAD and Railway. Deepened to 2 ft. by 1ft. 6 inches for length of 525 ft.

Ditch at I.11.a.7.4. Completed for 100 yards (ditch 2 ft. by 1ft. 6 inches).

"U" Trench near H.19. 105 yards deepened and widened, drained and prepared for "A" frames.

Railway Wood New Trench. 213 yards widened to 4 ft. at top and 2 ft. at bottom.

New Trench started in front of S.18.

Craters. Crater 2.A. Dugouts in crater taken down and entrance barricaded.
          Crater 1.A. Entrance barricaded.

Trench from Crater to Railway. Parapet and parados of rear lip of crater thickened.

I.11.b.6.6. 35 yards of communication trench completed, 30 yards partly completed.

WEST LANE. 50 yards parapet built up and repaired. Duck boards repaired.

X LINE. Bays 94 to 100 raised, parapet thickened with earth from borrow ditch, parapet built 100 ft. by 2 ft. by 2 ft. Anchorages put in near HAYMARKET.
In X.1 and 2 fire step improved and parapet thickened. The fitting of "A" frames and corrugated iron and the laying of trench boards commenced.

CABLE TRENCH. Near White Chateau - completed for 1000 yards.
West Lane Track. - Nearly completed.
Potijze Track. - Nearly completed.

PICCADILLY. - Western end. Line re-dug and "A" frames and galvanised iron revetments placed for 400 yards.
Trench connecting PICCADILLY and PARK LANE behind support line dug to a depth of 4 ft. 6 inches.
In PARK LANE the trench has been re-dug. "A" frames and galvanised iron revetting completed for 800 yards. Revetting with screens started at eastern end.

- 2 -

POTIJZE. 8 elephant shelters (covered in) ~~built~~.
Regimental aid post started.

WHITE CHATEAU   Second machine gun emplacement in hand.

LANCER FARM, HUSSAR FARM and DRAGOON FARM.   5 elephant shelters in course of construction.

ECOLE Strong Point.   Strutting completed, traversing half done, sandbagging commenced.

MENIN ROAD Barricade.   Steel shelter worked on ~~constructed~~ for machine gun.

LEFT SECTOR.

Firing Line.   Parapet and parados generally improved.
NEW JOHN STREET and from B.9 to B.12 and at A.7 and A.8, parados and traverses improved and revetted, and damage done by shells during the day repaired.

In Trench near JOHN STREET.   Much work done building up parapet and parados, revetting and fixing frames, and digging borrow ditch.

LA BRIQUE.   Trench improved.

Machine Gun Emplacements at C.28.d.3.2 and I.4.b.8.4 improved.

PROWSE FARM.   Machine Gun detachments' dug-out completed.

ST. JEAN.   4 large and one small shell proof shelters on.

MILL COTTAGES.   Heavy T.M. emplacements.   Ammunition gallery carried from shaft to emplacement.   2 sections elephant worked on

VINERY.   Excavation for one elephant completed.

DRAINAGE.   1500 yards BELLEWAARDEBEEK and 1700 yards of other drain cleaned.

KAAIE SALIENT.   Much work done rebuilding parapet and parados, and draining.   50 yards of fire step built.   105 yards boarded and 70 yards hurdle revetments placed and anchored.

RAMPARTS.   2 Chlorinating tanks worked on.

17th August, 1916.

Major-General,
Commanding 29th Division.

Headquarters,
VIII Corps.

Copy

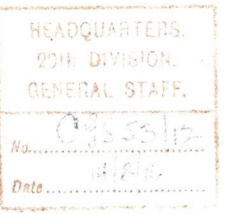

Work Report - 29th Division

Period ending 13/8/16

Right Sector.

<u>Firing Line</u> generally deepened and parapets built up and strengthened. Consolidating rear lip of crater No.6. H13 to H18 parapet raised and duck boards cleaned out Sap from 1 to 1 A deepened and widened.
Wire in front of H.19 and from the Gully to the Crater also in front of A 3 and for 40 yards to the left of Park Lane.
<u>Communication Trench,</u> along railway from A 1 to join Right Battalions.
Existing work improved and work continued.
<u>Communication Trench</u> in Gully widened to 2' at bottom sides revetted and Trench Boards laid.

<u>Duke Street.</u> Parapet built up and thickened.

<u>Haymarket.</u> Parapet revetted and thickened, trench boards repaired and bombing post constructed.

<u>X Line.</u> Much work deepening and building up parapets cleaning and replacing trench boards; building M.G. Emplacements and a borrow-trench in front.
All revetting and anchoring is now complete with exception of Bay 89.
<u>West Lane</u> Gaps in parapet have been built in.
<u>Dug-outs.</u> At Lancer Farm, and Dragoon Farm excavating. At Hussar Farm excavation complete and concreting commenced.

<u>Ecole and Menin Road.</u> Cellars Nos. 22,25,27,29,35,42, 43 and 46 being excavated, cleared and protected.

Left Sector.

<u>Firing Line</u> from B9 to B12 revetted and improved.
<u>Strand</u> Work continued, revetting and building up parapet.
<u>New St.John's Street.</u> Revetting continued.
<u>Congreve Walk.</u> Parapet and parados improved.
<u>New Trench</u> From St.John's Street to Wieltje is being built and revetted.
<u>Potizje Chateau and the vinery</u> Three dug-outs excavated and ready for concreting.
<u>Kaaie Salient.</u> Bridge repaired. Traverses and bays repaired.
<u>St. Jean.</u> Shelters erected in billets Numbers 3,5,12,13 and being erected in 12, and 14.
<u>Prowes Farm.</u> M.G. dug-out completed.

14th August, 1916.

Major General.
Commanding 29th Division

HEADQUARTERS,
29th DIVISION.
GENERAL STAFF.

C.G.S. 53/12.

Date............

Headquarters,
VIII Corps.

WORK REPORT.   29TH DIVISION
Period ending 9/8/16.

RIGHT SECTOR.   A great deal of work done in improving parapets. Wire on this front generally repaired and considerably improved. Trench Boards re-set and wired to prevent slipping.

Communication trenches considerably improved. New Communication trench dug behind Battalion Headquarters, Left Sub-sector.

Work continued on the new "X" Line, also on new trenches from No.4 Crater to Railway, and from behind No.1a Crater towards OUTPOST FARM.

WEST LANE Track I.8.d.3.6. - I.9.c.0.6. - I.9.d.25.30. - I.9.d.3.7. has been dug through and is complete except in a few places where bridges are required.

Dug-outs in houses on MENIN ROAD being worked at.

MENIN ROAD Camouflage screens repaired and new ones erected.

Extention of PICCADILLY to the new "X" line started, this trench is now ready to receive frames.

Elephants erected and partially prossfed, at POTIJZE CHATEAU, LANCER, HUSSAR, and DRAGOON FARM.

Machine Gun Emplacements MENIN GATE concreted.

ECOLE dug-outs.   Position occupied by Infantry Company, protection complete, strutting and traversing cellars in occupied portion being worked on.

Work on dug-outs for Field Ambulance (F.13) continued.

LEFT SECTOR.

LEFT SECTOR.   Parapets generally raised and thickened.

Wire considerably improved along whole front. Parados improved.

Prepared position in wall of WIELTJE FARM for Lewis Gun.

Wire and revetting material collected from various dumps and centralised.

C.28.d.20.35. Work started on emplacement for Machine Gun. Approach trench cleaned and made passable.

Light Trench Railway from CHURCH in ST JEAN STREET to trench B.11. repaired and put in good working order. This is now used for taking up material for front line.

POTIJZE Track dug from I.8.b.4.8. to I.3.central.

Revetting and flooring of trench at WIELTJE completed and handed over to C.R.E.

Work continued on Heavy Trench Mortar Emplacements. Dugout complete and proofed. 5' foot gallery completed.

Camouflage screens put up on POTIJZE ROAD, BRIELEN ROAD, ASYLUM.

Dug-out accomodation continued in YPRES.

Work continued on KAAIE SALIENT.

Trench from NEW ST JOHN'S ROAD to WIELTJE almost complete.

Four elephant dug-outs erected in ST JEAN. Cellars cleaned out and strutted, etc.

10th August 1916.

Major General,
Commanding 29th Division.

29TH DIVISION DAILY SUMMARY.

From 10 a.m. 31.8.16. to 10 a.m. 1.9.16.

OPERATIONS.

GAS. A full report on the gas attack carried out from our Right Sector has already been forwarded.

ARTILLERY.

The enemy's artillery was active yesterday afternoon firing several heavy shells behind OUTPOST FARM and in YPRES. ST. JEAN and B.11 also received attention during the morning.
In retaliation for our bombardment at night, enemy fired some 15 c.m. on our front trenches A.5.a. to A.8. inclusive, causing six casualties, but very little damage to our trenches.
Between 1.35 a.m. and 3 a.m. he also bombarded B.9. They also fired some light shells on MUDDY LANE and DUCK WALK commencing about 8 minutes after our first emission of gas.
Some 60 shells were fired into LA BRIQUE during the day.

Machine Guns. During the night the enemy machine guns were active as usual against ROULERS RAILWAY, and they enfiladed the following trenches from the North - X.5, X.4 and B.11.
Our Right Brigade reports that six or seven hostile machine guns kept up a slow rate of fire along our front during the gas attack.
Our own machine guns were particularly active last night, those in the Left Sector alone firing some 8500 rounds on to the enemy's front line and selected points behind it.

Trench Mortars. The enemy bombarded B.9 at 9.30 a.m. but however very soon stopped on our artillery retaliating. Our Stokes mortars fired a considerable number of rounds during the gas attack last night.

Patrols. Two patrols went out from our Right Sector after the gas attack and reported that the enemy were sending up Very lights about every second bay and though they could not get through the enemy's wire, they heard the enemy coughing a great deal, and they report that great excitement prevailed. An officer with one of these patrols reported that the enemy were running up and down the duckboards of the trench.

INTELLIGENCE.

Enemy Work. Work was heard close to KAISER BILL throughout the whole night in spite of our Lewis Gun fire.
By day sounds of bailing were heard.
Work still proceeds at OSKAR FARM, fresh earth having been thrown up in front of the parapet.

MISCELLANEOUS.

Flares. At 1.30 a.m. and again at 2.15 a.m. red flares were sent up by the enemy which broke into gold.

Smoke. Smoke was seen coming from the rear of OSKAR FARM at 7.30 a.m.

Aeroplanes. Considerable activity of anti-aircraft firing took place on both sides. At 10.30 a.m. a hostile aeroplane was driven back by two of our aeroplanes, and at 5.45 a.m. two more flew over the SALIENT but retired as soon as they were fired at.

1.9.16.

Major, G.S.,
29th Division.

29TH DIVISION DAILY SUMMARY.

From 10 a.m. 30.8.16. to 10 a.m. 31.8.16.

HEADQUARTERS.
D.S.134.
INTELLIGENCE.

OPERATIONS.

Artillery. Hostile artillery generally inactive except for slight retaliation with 77 mm. on MONMOUTH TRENCH for bombardment by our trench mortars at 5 p.m. A few shrapnel burst over the STRAND at 7 p.m.

Machine Guns. Usual amount of machine gun fire was directed by the enemy along ROULERS RAILWAY. An enemy machine gun fires from I.5.b.95.10. Our machine guns fired on VON HUGEL FARM (C.23.d), BRIDGE HOUSE (C.23.a), JASPER FARM (C.23.b) and the trench tramways in C.23.a. They also traversed enemy's third line trench in I.6.a. and I.6.c. Our Lewis guns fired on a party of the enemy which was observed to be working in KAISER BILL at 3 p.m. The gunners claim to have killed five of the party. Our Lewis guns also fired at intervals on enemy working parties heard near KAISER BILL and the MOUND, during the night.

Trench Mortars. Our Stokes Mortars bombarded ARGYLL FARM (C.28.b.8.9) between 4 p.m. and 6 p.m., two of the enemy had been reported there.

Our 2" trench mortars fired several rounds at the enemy front line trench between C.29.a.3.9 and C.29.a.4.7.

Snipers. Enemy snipers were more active than usual. An enemy sniper is suspected in hedge near I.5.b.6.1. but his exact position has not yet been located.

INTELLIGENCE.

Enemy Work. Enemy wire immediately South of KAISER BILL appears to have been strengthened.
Enemy's wire considerably strengthened and about 20 iron screw posts are visible about I.12.a.3.2.
A party of the enemy could be heard talking in trenches opposite No.2 Crater. They were apparently cleaning up trench, as water could be seen being thrown over the parapet.

MISCELLANEOUS.

Lights. Rather more flares were sent up by the enemy than usual.

Aeroplanes. Three enemy aeroplanes came over our line at about 8.50 a.m., but were immediately driven back by our anti-aircraft guns.

31.8.16.

Major, G.S.,
29th Division.

D.S.133

HEADQUARTERS
29th DIVISION
INTELLIGENCE

No.......
Date......

29TH DIVISION DAILY SUMMARY.
From 10 a.m. 29.8.16. to 10 a.m. 30.8.16.

OPERATIONS.

Artillery. Enemy's artillery were inactive except for a few small shells in the direction of HUSSAR FARM (I.4.c.7.7) and POTIJZE.

Machine Guns. Enemy's machine guns very active during the night in our right sector, the chief targets being along ROULERS RAILWAY, F.11 and HELLFIRE CORNER. Our machine guns traversed the enemy third line between C.23.a.3.2 and VERLORENHOEK, the road fork in C.23.a, and also VON HUGEL FARM and adjacent trenches in square C.23.d.

GAS. At 10.30 p.m. a Gas Alarm was sounded by the Division on our right, but no gas was felt on our front.

INTELLIGENCE. NIL.

MISCELLANEOUS.

Signals. About the time of the Gas Alarm (10.30 p.m.) two green rockets and a number of white flares went up from the direction from which the alarm originated. (It is presumed that these were our own.)

The whole of this period has been particularly quiet.

30.8.16.

Major, G.S.,
29th Division.

29th DIVISION DAILY SUMMARY

From 10 a.m. 28.8.16 to 10 a.m. 29t8.16

D.S. 132.

OPERATIONS.

Artillery.   Enemy artillery very quiet. A few large shells were fired into "HELLFIRE CORNER" and a few burst over X 8 about 27.d.7.6. causing some casualties. Our guns retaliated on enemy front line doing considerable damage to his sap opposite Crater No. 2a I.12.a.1.0. Enemy fired a few high velocity shells into RAILWAY Trench and along the Railway. POTIJZE VILLAGE also received some attention.

Machine Guns.   Enemy machine guns were specially active between 10-30 and 11 p.m. south of "KAISER BILL" otherwise normal. Our machine guns fired close on 4,000 rounds on various targets in C 23 B and D and also at BRIDGE House C 24 a.

Patrol (1).   A patrol went out from I.5.b.2.0. to a point about 200 yards in front of our wire. No enemy patrols were met but work could be plainly heard all along his front line, it sounded like wire frames being driven in.
Patrol (2).   A patrol of 1 Officer and 8 other ranks went out from C.29.c.6.8. at about 9-30 p.m. and returned about mid-night. Enemy was heard working north of the MOUND.
Nothing further to report.

INTELLIGENCE.

At 5.55 p.m. two men were seen walking in the direction of OSCAR FARM I.6.c.0.9. in grey uniforms and caps. Enemy was heard working near L.R.B. Cottage C.23.c.0.2.

MISCELLANEOUS.

Aeroplanes.   Between 9a.m. and 9-30 p.m. (28th instant) a hostile aeroplane dropped a few bombs round gun position to the south of HASLER HOUSE C.27.d.4.3. Another plane flew over X 3 at 6-30 p.m. same date but was driven back. It dropped a rocket which broke into White Stars.

RIFLE GRENADES.   At about 4-30 a.m. the enemy fired a few rifle grenades along the whole front of our Right Sector.

29.8.16.

Major. G.S.,

29th Division.

D.S.131.

29TH DIVISION DAILY SUMMARY.

From 10 a.m. 27.8.16. to 10 a.m. 28.8.16.

OPERATIONS.

Artillery. Enemy artillery very quiet during this period. A few shells were fired into POTIJZE at 5.30 p.m. and along the POTIJZE ROAD at 7.30 p.m. A few shrapnel shells were fired over YPRES at about 10 p.m. MONMOUTH TRENCH and B.10 also received a little attention.

Machine Guns. Enemy machine gun activity normal. Our machine guns fired on enemy trench tramway between C.22.b.90.58 and C.23.a.78.63, also on the road and tramway junction in C.24.a. and on possible battery at C.24.a.2.8, SPREE FARM in C.18.d. and adjacent cross roads, and the trench tramway junction near JASPER FARM in C.29.b.5.8.

Trench Mortars. Enemy trench mortars inactive. Our trench mortars fired a few rounds during the night.

Snipers - were quiet all day.

Patrols. (1) An officer's patrol consisting of 1 officer and 7 other ranks, left C.28.b.63.88 at 11.30 p.m. and moved along the northern side of the WIELTJE - ST. JULIEN ROAD to C.22.d.7.3. No enemy patrols were seen or heard. A machine gun was firing either from WELL COTTAGE (C.22.d.98.52) or from point C.23.c.10.61. They also reported that the gun firing on MONMOUTH TRENCH as above reported appeared to be situated somewhere on the WIELTJE - ST. JULIEN ROAD not far behind the enemy front line approximately at C.23.a.5.4. This patrol found a dead German lying in a shell hole on our side of the wire at C.28.b.60.88. The body had ~~apparently~~ probably lain there from two to five days. He belonged to the 236th R.I.R., the shoulder strap is forwarded herewith (There were also found on him a notebook and a 5-mark note both of which have been handed over to the Lieut-Colonel i/c of Intelligence Second Army). He had 6 ordinary German hand grenades in his possession. The patrol returned at 2.50 a.m.

(2) An officer's patrol of 1 N.C.O. and 3 men went out to ODER HOUSE at 10 p.m., returning at 11.15 p.m. without having heard or seen anything suspicious.

INTELLIGENCE.

Enemy Work. Enemy were heard hammering in wooden stakes at C.23.c.25.10 approximately.
Enemy were also heard hammering in stakes in the vicinity of ODER HOUSE.
A small party of the enemy were seen working about I.6.c.1.3 in round green hats with light coloured bands.

Enemy Movements. At various times during the day men in twos and threes were moving about at C.30.d.4.7. They did not appear to be carrying anything.

MISCELLANEOUS.

Four Very lights were sent up at irregular intervals from the junction of saps at C.22.d.77.52.
Aeroplane activity considerably below normal.

Major, G.S.,
29th Division.

28.8.16.

D.S. 130.

29TH DIVISION DAILY SUMMARY.
From 10 a.m. 26.8.16. to 10 a.m. 27.8.16.

OPERATIONS.

Artillery. Enemy's artillery has shown rather more activity during the last 24 hours. Particular attention was paid to RAILWAY WOOD and H.15 on both of which he fired bursts at intervals. He ceased fire on every occasion as soon as our guns retaliated. Other points shelled were :- MONMOUTH TRENCH, JOHN STREET, WIELTJE - ST. JEAN ROAD, GARDEN STREET, Trenches A.1, X.2, and HAYMARKET. Little damage was however done.

Machine Guns. Little activity in our right sector. More than usual firing on both sides in our left sector, the enemy sweeping the front from WIELTJE SALIENT (inclusive) to C.29.a.4.0., and he also searched ST. JEAN - WIELTJE ROAD. Our machine guns fired 4000 rounds on targets in C.23.c. & d., on CORNER COTTAGE in C.17.b. and SPREE FARM in C.18.b.

Trench Mortars. Little trench mortar activity is reported. Three small bombs were fired near B.9.

Patrols. An officers' patrol left C.28.b.65.85 and proceeded along the ST. JULIEN ROAD to the COTTAGE at C.22.d.65.10. Distinct tracks were seen along the East side of the road and in the direction of the enemy's lines. At the bend in the road at C.22.d.6.3 they noticed long grass was well trodden down. It is thought that this point is a rendezvous of the enemy's patrols. No hostile patrol was encountered. A machine gun was firing from C.22.d.3.2 in the direction approximately over the small pond at the bend of the road at C.22.d.6.3.
Other patrols report work seen about OSKAR FARM and work heard at I.5.d.10.7.

INTELLIGENCE.

Enemy Work. A large working party was heard driving in stakes just north of the MOUND. Enemy also reported working at I.12.c.57.10 and sap at I.12.c.8.5 (fresh earth observed here) and in the neighbourhood of C.29.a.5.6.

Enemy Movements. At 5 p.m. two men observed in front line wearing grey uniforms and caps with red bands.
A man on horseback was observed to approach house near Railway Station at J.1.a.
6 men were seen to leave the same building and go to the STATION BUILDINGS. 3 of these men were in grey uniform, and caps with red bands. The other 3 wore dark uniforms. Two bell tents were pitched in front of STATION BUILDINGS and considerable activity was observed.

MISCELLANEOUS.

At 8.45 p.m. several red lights were seen going up near YPRES from the northern sub-sector. The enemy immediately sent over several shells which appeared to burst over YPRES.

Major, G.S.,

27.8.16.   29th Division.

D.S.129.

29TH DIVISION DAILY SUMMARY.

From 10 a.m. 25.8.16. to 10 a.m. 26.8.16.

OPERATIONS.

Artillery. Enemy artillery has been more active during this period. At about 9.30 a.m. about 15 H.E. and shrapnel were fired on POTIJZE Road at about I.3.d.10.9. At 9.50 a.m. the batteries about SAVILE Road were shrapnelled. At 10 a.m. a few trench mortar bombs were fired on ROULERS Railway at I.11.b.7.8. A few high velocity shells were fired into a point about I.5.d.3.4.

Machine Guns. Enemy machine guns very active between 10 p.m. and midnight. Five hostile machine guns swept the WIELTJE Salient and B.9, also the road between WIELTJE and ST. JEAN.
Our machine guns retaliated on BOSSAERT FARM (C.23.b.1.5), ST. JULIEN Road (C.23.a), and also between BOSSAERT FARM and ST. JULIEN Road (C.23.a).

Patrols.
(1) A patrol went out from I.5.b.0.5 at 11 p.m. and reports that the wire at the MOUND is the ordinary low entanglements about five yards in depth at a distance of about 20 yards from enemy trench. Patrol got to within 20 yards of the wire in question, which is thick and strong.
(2) Another patrol went out from H.17 (I.12.c.1.9). They report enemy wiring at point 67 (I.12.c.6.7).
(3) Another patrol went out from I.5.d.2.9 at 9.45 p.m. and took up position about 100 yards from our wire. Sounds of iron being dumped behind OSKAR FARM were heard, also hammering and shovelling about I.5.b.10.0.

INTELLIGENCE.

Enemy's lines very quiet and there is nothing to report beyond that mentioned under Patrols.

MISCELLANEOUS.

Signals. Between KAISER BILL and WIELTJE-FORTUIN Road between 11 p.m. and midnight, two red rockets were sent up by the enemy. Nothing followed.
Fewer flares than usual were put up between KAISER BILL (C.29.a.8.1) and EITEL FRITZ FARM (I.5.b.7.7).

Aeroplanes. At about 10.45 a.m. a British plane was brought down in enemy's lines opposite A.1.

Major, G.S.,
29th Division.

26.8.16.

D.S.128.

29TH DIVISION DAILY SUMMARY.

From 10 a.m. 24.8.16. to 10 a.m. 25.8.16.

OPERATIONS.

Artillery. Enemy artillery particularly quiet during this period. MUD LANE and New Trench from Railway Barricade were shelled slightly in the evening.
B.9 was slightly shelled between 1 a.m. and 2 a.m.

Machine Guns. Enemy machine guns were active at "stand to" in the morning.
Our machine guns fired over 2000 rounds at various targets including Cross Roads in C.23.c., BOSSAERT FARM and adjoining road and communication trench (C.23.b) and Forked roads C.23.a.

Trench Mortars. A small enemy trench mortar interfered with work at B.9 about 1.30 a.m. causing two casualties. Also a few light trench mortar bombs were thrown at H.20 at about 11.40 p.m.

Snipers. Enemy's snipers particularly quiet.

Patrols. (1) A patrol of 1 officer and 3 men went out to examine enemy saps near Crater No.4 (I.11.b). Enemy heard working near the end of the sap.
(2) A patrol went out from I.5.d.2.8 at about 11 p.m. Enemy heard driving stakes at about I.6.a.0.9½. Also horse transport was heard along the road north of ROULERS Railway. No enemy patrols were seen.
(3) A patrol of 1 officer and 4 other ranks left trench B.9 at about 9.30 p.m. and proceeded up the ditch some 60 yards towards the enemy's lines. An enemy listening patrol was found, they gradually retired as our patrol advanced. On reaching the position held by the enemy's listening post, grass was found all beaten down, proving that the enemy are in the habit of keeping a listening post at this spot. Our patrol returned about midnight. Strength of enemy's listening post estimated at 4 men.

INTELLIGENCE.

Enemy Work. At 11.45 p.m. a small enemy working party was seen near the MOUND (I.5.b). On completion of the work, a white flag was put up and left.
At 6.45 a.m. 4 men were seen about I.5.b.9.1 putting sandbags on the parados and driving in stakes.
New sandbags also visible at I.5.d.9.9.

Enemy Movements. At 1.45 a.m. a small party of the enemy came up against our line near Crater No.6 (I.11.b). They were fired on by a Lewis Gun and bombed. Enemy replied with about 30 bombs. No damage done on either side.

MISCELLANEOUS.

One of the enemy in grey uniform with small cap and white band supposed to have been seen at I.12.a.6.0. He was fired at and believed to have been hit.

Another man in grey uniform with green shoulder straps and green chako was seen to enter a suspected emplacement or O.P. at I.12.a.6.2.

Aeroplanes very active during the evening on both sides.

Lights. At 11.15 p.m. towards KAISER BILL large white star with small white one falling from it was seen, also a red rocket breaking into white stars in the direction of HOOGE.

Major,
G.S., 29th Division.

25.8.16.

D.S.127.

29TH DIVISION DAILY SUMMARY.
From 10 a.m. 23.8.16. to 10 a.m. 24.8.16.

OPERATIONS.

Artillery. The enemy's artillery not been exceptionally active during this period. A few H.E. and shrapnel were fired into POTIJZE Road and SAVILLE Road about 8.15 a.m.

Machine Guns. Very little activity shewn by the enemy machine guns. Our machine guns fired over 2000 rounds on the following targets :- C.23.d.0.3 - C.23.d.4.6 - the Cross Roads at C.23.c.9.5 and BOESAERT FARM together with road and adjoining communication trench.

Snipers. An enemy sniper observed behind tree stump 20 yards South of ARGYLL FARM. Claim to have been hit by one of our snipers.
F.12 and RAILWAY FARM constantly sniped at long range.

Patrols. A patrol of the 16th Middlesex went out from I.5.d.5.3 at 12.30 a.m. in the direction of I.6.c.½.3. At 1.25 a.m. enemy were heard wiring near that spot. Patrol returned and got Lewis Gun turned on to enemy wiring party. Work ceased.
    Another patrol of the 16th Middlesex went out at 12.45 a.m. from I.5.d.2½.7 to a point just beyond our own wire. At 1.25 a.m. sounds of work were heard from a point just north of the MOUND, and also in front of RITEL FRITZ FARM.

INTELLIGENCE.

Enemy Work. South of KAISER BILL sawing of wood and sounds of timber being moved could be heard. North of KAISER BILL little was heard except sounds of metal being dumped near WHITE COTTAGE.

Train Activity. Train reported travelling from south to north near STATION Buildings I.10.a.2.0 at 6.30 p.m. Stationery train seen at C.29.b.45.50.

MISCELLANEOUS.

Very few flares were put up in this part of the sector and the quiet which prevailed may point to a relief having taken place.
Enemy aeroplane flew low over X.3 at 6 p.m.

Enemy sent up red flares at 10 p.m. and 11 p.m. and one red and one white at 2.25 a.m. Nothing followed.

Major, G.S.,
29th Division.

24.8.16.

D.S.126.

29TH DIVISION DAILY SUMMARY.

From 10 a.m. 22.8.16. to 10 a.m. 23.8.16.

HEADQUARTERS,
29th DIVISION,
GENERAL STAFF.

No.............
Date............

OPERATIONS.

Artillery. At 8.15 a.m. about a dozen rounds of H.E. were dropped on POTIJZE, and at 5 p.m. a few H.E. on SAVILE ROAD. A few H.E. shrapnel burst over POTIJZE WOOD (Battalion Headquarters) at 8.15.
HASLER HOUSE (Battalion Headquarters and O.P.) received special attention during the period, being fired at with 7.7 c.m. and 10.5 c.m. as well as a H.V. gun.
Other targets were B.10 at 1.30 p.m., the path between ST. JEAN and CANAL between 5.45 p.m. and 7.15 p.m., and during the night MONMOUTH TRENCH.

Trench Mortars. A 7.5 LEICHTE WURF-MINE gas (?) shell case found in left sector is forwarded.

Machine Guns. Rather more active than usual.
This was especially noticeable in POTIJZE WOOD which was heavily fired on between 12.30 a.m. and 1 a.m.
POTIJZE ROAD was enfiladed from the N.E. at 10 p.m.
An automatic rifle - described as a "LEWIS GUN" - is reported to have fired from Sap at C.23.c.20.13 (observed from junction of NEW JOHN STREET and FIRING LINE).
Our guns fired at suspected ration dump at C.24.b.4.2 and at C.24.d.4.2.

Snipers. Snipers more active on right of Divisional Line.

Patrols. (a) An officer's patrol left AIR STREET at 10.55 keeping just N. of GULLY. Heard work about I.6.c.2.4 as of driving in stakes, and returned at midnight.
(b) A sergeant and two men left I.5.d.3.6 and went to within 150 yards of the German line. Work seemed to be in progress about I.6.c.0.8 (driving in stakes and emptying of trenches [trucks] of what might be concrete) and at I.5.b.5.3 (dumping iron sheets and much whistling and singing).
(c) Officers patrol left C.29.a.50.05 at 11 p.m. but could not proceed more than 20 yards beyond our wire owing to machine gun fire.

INTELLIGENCE.

Enemy Movements. A man wearing grey uniform, green shoulder stripe [straps] and a helmet is reported to have been seen in enemy front trench opposite our right and another in a white topped cap in support line.
A sniper in NO MANS LAND (Left sector position not stated) observed an Officer taking a bath at the junction of the Saps at C.22.d.8.6 where about 12 men were working at the time. As the sniper could not communicate, no action was taken.
At 4.45 p.m. a train of about 4 coaches was seen on the WESTHOEK - FREZENBERG Road proceeding from S. to N. towards STATION Buildings.

Enemy Work. Enemy again working at I.12.a.0.4.
One party was fired at by Lewis Gun, cries were heard and no further work done.
Enemy also heard working at I.12.c.5.7.
Work and noise at, and N. and S. of KAISER BILL continues at night and during the early morning. Knife rests are visible in the trenches and earth has been noticed being thrown up.

MISCELLANEOUS.

<u>Signals.</u>　At 9.30 p.m. a white rocket which burst into white stars went up from the direction of HAMPSHIRE FARM C.22.a.　Soon afterwards a large number of bombs were heard to go off near CAVAN STREET about 200 yards N.W. of junction with PRATT STREET.

23.8.16.

Capt.
for Major, G.S.,
29th Division.

D.S.125.

29TH DIVISION DAILY SUMMARY.

From 10 a.m. 21.8.16. to 10 a.m. 22.8.16.

OPERATIONS.

Artillery. Enemy's artillery retaliated with shrapnel and H.E. to our bombardment which began at 3 p.m. A certain amount of damage was done to our front line and support trenches notably :-
(1) A.8) Both of these sections
(2) B.9) completely blown in.
(3) The junction of B.11 and B.12 for part of B.11 immediately S.W. of the road in C.28.a.
In B.10 Salient a Lewis Gun and team were knocked out. Hostile trench mortars did most destruction and flattened out considerable stretches of the trenches between NEW JOHN STREET and the WIELTJE - FORTUIN Road.
A few casualties were caused.
The front and support trenches in the Right Sector (Right sub-sector) were shelled for some minutes at 3.15 p.m. and 8.30 p.m. little damage was done.
HAYMARKET, THE GULLY and No.6 Crater also received attention. The batteries at SAVILE Road and the CANAL Bank were also shelled.

Machine Guns. Enemy machine guns were active during the night.
Our own machine guns fired at various targets in C.23, 24 and 29.

Trench Mortars. Our trench mortars took part at the beginning of our bombardment.
Enemy trench mortars fired about 8 rounds at B.9 at 7.30 p.m. but stopped apparently because of our artillery retaliation.

Patrols. A patrol of the Middlesex Regiment (1 sergeant and 2 men) went out from A.5 in a N.E. direction. They heard enemy working party at the MOUND wiring and repairing, also sounds of iron being dumped probably at OSKAR FARM.
No hostile patrols seen.

INTELLIGENCE.

Enemy Work. During the night and early morning the enemy was working noisely, shouting and talking, and moving things about. This party was between KAISER BILL inclusive and the WIELTJE - FORTUIN ROAD in enemy front line system. Working party was detected behind WELL COTTAGE (C.23.c.0.5½) three Lewis guns were at once turned on to it and the party dispersed.
Enemy working party heard at I.12.a.0.4, our Lewis guns fired bursts at them during the night.

Enemy Movements. Horse transport was heard about 4.30 a.m. at I.6.c.4.5 north of ROULERS Railway.
Suspected enemy O.P. at C.30.c.6.9 in a tree which appears to have a revolving top.
There was an encounter between an enemy and Canadian patrol at 12.40 a.m. in front of OUTPOST FARM. The enemy was bombed by the Canadians and by No.1 post of the Lancashire Fusiliers.

MISCELLANEOUS.

Signals. At 1.15 a.m. a signal lamp was observed in enemy's lines about VERLORENHOEK, and a searchlight some little distance East of HOOGE.
Dumps. A dump is suspected at I.6.b near WILDE COTTAGE. A bombing post is suspected at I.5.b.3.5.

Major, G.S.
29th Division.

22.8.16.

D.S.124.

29TH DIVISION DAILY SUMMARY.

From 10 a.m. 20.8.16. to 10 a.m. 21.8.16.

OPERATIONS.

Artillery. At 10 p.m. enemy dropped 4 shells on the MENIN ROAD about 100 yards E. of HELL FIRE CORNER, 3 were "blind". The fourth appeared to be a "universal" fired from a long distance.
At 11 a.m. enemy fired a few H.E. on CRUMP FARM and on front line in I.11.b.
Between 5 p.m. and 6 p.m. several small shells landed at BATH HOUSE (I.4.a.6.5) and near SAVILE ROAD.
At 1.30 p.m. a few rounds of 10.5 and 7.7 c.m. were fired at our front line about C.29.a.2.2.
During the day some shelling was directed against the CANAL BANK in I.1.b. Several blinds were noticed.
At 10.30 a slow bombardment with small shells commenced against the WIELTJE SALIENT.
A few rounds were fired at GARDEN STREET between 3.45 p.m. and 4.30 p.m.

Machine Guns. Enemy machine guns were active on the Left Sector.

Snipers. Quiet. A sniper was detected from C.28.b.70.85 at C.29.a.1.8 but no action was taken as we had parties out at the time.

Patrols. 2 patrols went out on our front.
(a) Went out from C.29.d.0.0 at 10.30.
The patrol ascertained that a trench supposed to run from ODER HOUSE to the German lines at C.29.d.4.0 is in reality a bank with a small ditch at the bottom which affords good cover from view. The grass at the bottom of the ditch was well trodden down and the ditch is apparently frequently used.
The patrol also discovered some German bombs on our wire and two German bodies.
Report and List of identifications herewith.
(b) Went out from I.11.b.70.95 towards I.6.c.1.0. Saw nothing of enemy and returned at 1 a.m.

INTELLIGENCE.

Enemy Work. About 12 of the enemy were seen working on their second line trench at I.6.a.2.3 at 12.30 p.m.
A party were seen carrying planks to the MOUND from the fire trench at 3.25 p.m.
Enemy working parties seen at I.12.c.0.4 at 11.30 p.m. and 1.30, were dispersed by Lewis Gun fire.

MISCELLANEOUS.

At 11.5 p.m. a white flare breaking into white stars was sent up from I.12.c.5.7. Nothing followed.

2 searchlights were visible in the direction of BELLEWAARDE FARM at 11 p.m. and 11.12 p.m.

Major, G.S.,

21.8.16.   29th Division.

List of articles found on a dead German Soldier at C 29.d.1.0
night 20/21 August 1916.
----

1. Identity Disc.   Adam Strauss
                                    Andenhausen 27.8.96
                                    11. Ers. B H   J.R. 167
                                       R.I.R. 234   6K
                                              599

2. Soldbuch.
3. Feldgesaugbuch.
4. Case marked H.F. Waldschmit Nacht (ordinary cigar case with seller's name.)
5. Feldpostbrief.
6. Schutzbrief.   Dubious. This was picked up in our trench in daylight near the spot where the body lay. It was not actually taken off the dead man.
7. Wirecutters.
8. German hand grenade.   6 were carried.   Specimen herewith (harmless)
9. Rifle.   Marked R.J.R. 234 - 6 K 75.
10. Bayonet and Scabbard.
11. Automatic pistol and holster   6294 d   (1916)

Headquarters,
    87th Brigade.

Articles, as per attached list, were taken off the body of a dead German brought in last night by one of our patrols.
On taking over these lines from the 2nd. Royal Fusiliers they reported that on night of 17th instant one of their Lewis Guns fired on two Germans who were tying bombs on to our wire and missed them. They left the bombs on the wire. Yesterday afternoon, whilst these bombs were being examined from the front line trenches two dead Germans were seen on our wire within about 25 yards of the bombs. Their bodies were brought in last night and buried. One had no identification at all on him, neither of them had any hats. The identity disc and other articles herewith were taken off the other body. Everything points to these two men being the men fired on by the Fusiliers on the night of the 17th instant.
If the revolver and rifle are not required, the officer who retrieved the bodies would like to have them if practicable.

                                        (Signed) A. J. WELCH,
                                                Lieut-Colonel,
                                        Commanding 1st K.O.S.B.

D.S.123.

29TH DIVISION DAILY SUMMARY.

From 10 a.m. 19.8.16. to 10 a.m. 20.8.16.

OPERATIONS.

Artillery. About 1 p.m. enemy threw a few H.E. shells on H.21 and three near RAILWAY FARM at 1.30 p.m.
At about 10.30 a.m. (19th instant) 12 rounds of 10.5 c.m. were fired at the ST. JEAN - YPRES Road 50 yards out of ST. JEAN.
During the morning (20th instant) about 9 7.7 landed in the WIELTJE Salient being fired at intervals of 10 minutes.

Trench Mortars. 2 or 3 trench mortar bombs were thrown on the ROULERS Railway near A.1 at 7.15 p.m. and at 11 p.m.

Machine Guns. Between midnight and 1 a.m. the enemy enfiladed the WIELTJE Road with Machine gun fire.

Snipers. - Quiet.

INTELLIGENCE.

Enemy Movements. About 1.45 a.m. an enemy patrol was seen 20 yards from our wire at A.4. It was fired upon without success.

Enemy Work. At 10 a.m. two men were seen carrying timber in enemy front line, just N. of ROULERS Railway.
At 1.30 a.m. sounds of enemy working parties in trenches opposite were heard at H.20.

Patrols. Two officers patrols went out during the night.
(a) Left our trench at 11 p.m. from A.4, returning at 12.45 a.m. They found no signs of enemy patrols but heard shouting and sounds of work at the MOUND.
(b) Left crater No. 1.A at 11.30 p.m. and reached enemy's sap at I.6.c.1.5, returning at 1.30 a.m. They neither saw nor heard anything of the enemy.

MISCELLANEOUS.

A train was heard at 11 a.m. (19th instant) in front of the Left Sector.

A trolley was heard at 5 a.m. (20th instant) in the direction of the MOUND.

Major, G.S.,

20th August, 1916.   29th Division.

D.S.122.

29TH DIVISION DAILY SUMMARY.

From 10 a.m. 18.8.16. to 10 a.m. 19.8.16.

OPERATIONS.

Artillery. The enemy's artillery displayed slight activity during this period. Front line in the neighbourhood of WARWICK FARM and CRUMP FARM were shelled from about 9 a.m. to 11 a.m. Trenches from A.8 to WIELTJE were shelled at 10.30 a.m., 2.30 p.m. and 4.30 p.m. YPRES - ST. JEAN - WIELTJE Road received attention at about 10 a.m.

Snipers very quiet.

Machine Guns. Enemy machine guns active (I.5.b.1.2 to C.29.a.1½.3½) from 1 a.m. to 1.30 a.m. and from C.29.a.1½.3½ to WIELTJE at "Stand to", also occasional bursts on MONMOUTH TRENCH.

Patrols. Two patrols of 2nd Royal Fusiliers went out on either side of the VERLORENHOEK Road. Nothing was seen of the enemy but work was heard going on.
A patrol of 1 officer, 1 sergeant and 3 men left at 10.30 p.m. from C.29.a.25.15. They reached the German wire, where they found a wiring party, working very systematically and quietly. The covering party approached within 10 yards of them but did not see them. They appeared to be very uneasy. Beyond the wiring party was another working with zinc sheets, apparently in their front trench.
1 N.C.O. and 3 men also went out at 10.30 p.m. from C.29.c.6.6. They went forward about 150 yards and hid in a shell hole. About 1.30 a.m. enemy patrol of 3 or 4 men approached, but were fired on and retired at once - one man believed wounded. This patrol returned at 2 a.m.
A patrol went out from the Left sub-sector but saw no signs of enemy patrols.

INTELLIGENCE.

Enemy Movements. One of the enemy was observed from A.8 during the morning. He was wearing a white cap band. Between 4 p.m. and 6 p.m. three parties of 5 men each appeared near MOUSE TRAP FARM and reappeared carrying bags.

Enemy Work. Working party heard about C.23.c.3.6.

MISCELLANEOUS.

Pigeons observed over Left Sector (R. Sub-sector), one at 10.35 flying N.W., another at 10.50 flying S.

Enemy seen signalling with a white flag at 12.30 p.m. near MOUSE TRAP FARM.

19.8.16.

Major, G.S.,
29th Division.

D.S.121.

29TH DIVISION DAILY SUMMARY.

From 10 a.m. 17.8.16. to 10 a.m. 18.8.16.

OPERATIONS.

Artillery. SUNKEN ROAD and NEW TRENCH at I.12.c.1.6 were shelled at 7 p.m. and again at 8.30 p.m. apparently with 5.9's.
Between 5 p.m. and 6.30 p.m. an occasional H.E. shell fell near ST. JEAN. At 7.30 p.m. several H.E. shells landed near ST. JEAN and along the ST. JEAN - YPRES Road.
At 1 a.m. the enemy fired 6 rounds of shrapnel into MONMOUTH TRENCH (New Trench at C.29.b.) causing 12 casualties.
From 8 a.m. to 10 a.m. CAVAN TRENCH was shelled by field guns.

Machine Guns. Enemy's machine guns near WIELTJE were active from 2 a.m. to 2.30 a.m.

Snipers were very quiet.

INTELLIGENCE.

Enemy Movements. At 10.30 a.m. 7 men were seen carrying some shiny object to HAMPSHIRE FARM.
At 11.30 a.m. 2 men carried some heavy object from HAMPSHIRE FARM.
At 1.30 p.m. 12 men went to HAMPSHIRE FARM and came out later carrying loads on their backs; two carrying a box about 4 ft. 6 inches long.
HAMPSHIRE FARM was shelled by us from 4.15 p.m. to 5 p.m.
At 7.30 a party of 50 men was seen moving in a N.N.W. direction from MOUSE TRAP FARM.
Transport was heard at 7.55 a.m. apparently moving in a northerly direction from about RUPPRECHT FARM to about JASPER FARM.
The usual train activity was heard during the night.

Enemy Work. Enemy working parties were heard about I.12.a.3.1 during the early part of the night.
At 11 p.m. a German was seen to get over his wire about I.11.b.9.4 and crawl towards our wire. A bomb was thrown at him and he retired apparently wounded.
Last night and early this morning continuous hammering and sawing of wood could be heard going on near the MOUND.
These sounds are similar to those heard the night preceding the last emission of gas.
Enemy was heard working during the early morning near C.29.a.8.3.
New work was visible at KAISER BILL.

Patrols. At 2.30 a.m. two men having been reported in front of our wire at ODER HOUSE (C.29.d.3.0) a patrol went out but failed to find any trace of them.
The patrol however found in a disused trench 2 hand grenades of the usual type with their strings tied together and a wire running back from them to the German trenches, apparently a trap.
A wiring party reports that a large ditch about 8 x wide filled with water extends nearly all round Crater No.2

MISCELLANEOUS.

At 6.15 a pigeon was seen to fly over our lines near WARWICK FARM, flying from E to W.

Major, G.S.,
29th Division.

18.8.16.

D.S.120.

29TH DIVISION DAILY SUMMARY.
From 10 a.m. 16.8.16. to 10 a.m. 17.8.16.

OPERATIONS.

Artillery. Enemy artillery was active on the right sector. Salvos of 77 mm. shells were fired at 4 p.m., 7 p.m. and 12 midnight, 3.45 a.m. and 5 a.m. against No.2 crater, R.19 and the SUNKEN ROAD. Little damage was done.
At 2 p.m. and at 4.30 p.m. B.9 to B.10 was shelled by field guns.
Between 5.30 p.m. and 6.20 p.m. 4 5.9 shells landed near CAVAN TRENCH and N. end of NEW JOHN STREET and NEW TRENCH.
At 3.30 p.m. in reply to our fire enemy shelled POTIJZE with 5.9s and NEW JOHN STREET and GARDEN STREET with field guns.

Trench Mortars and Rifle Grenades. Enemy fired 4 rifle grenades from the vicinity of KAISER BILL at 11 p.m. We replied with 12 from A.8. Enemy retaliated with 30 trench mortar bombs, doing little damage.

Machine Guns. At 12.10 a.m. and 12.15 a.m. enemy fired bursts of machine gun fire over HELL FIRE CORNER.
On our left sector bursts of fire were directed at the parapet throughout the night.

Snipers. Snipers were noticeably less active along the whole front.

INTELLIGENCE.

Enemy Movements. Enemy were heard working at WHITE COTTAGE. Singing was heard near KAISER BILL.
At 10 p.m. shouting was heard at the same place and shortly afterwards a machine gun opened on our parapet. Working parties (apparently wiring) were heard from ODER HOUSE to the MOUND.
An enemy working party was apparently caught by our artillery fire at the gas alarm. Groaning of wounded could be plainly heard opposite the right of the Divisional line.

MISCELLANEOUS.

Aeroplanes. At about 11 p.m. an aeroplane crossed our lines dropping two small bombs near A.8 bay 11. and at 11.40 p.m. another bomb was dropped near the ECOLE.
At 12.15 a.m. a bomb was dropped in rear of the left of the Divisional line.
No damage is reported.

17.8.16.

Major, G.S.,
29th Division.

D.S.119.

29TH DIVISION DAILY SUMMARY.

From 10 a.m. 15.8.16. to 10 a.m. 16.8.16.

OPERATIONS.

Artillery. At 11.30 a.m. about 30 77 c.m. shells were fired at Support Trenches in CAMBRIDGE ROAD near the Railway.
Enemy also fired at the DUCK WALK about 5 p.m.
The WHITE CHATEAU was again shelled with 5.9's at 2 p.m.
Between 3.30 p.m. and 4.30 p.m. enemy dropped about 12 shells into POTIJZE.
During the morning I.8.a.4.4 to I.8.a.9.9 was shelled with 5.9's.

Trench Mortars. Enemy's mortars fired at A.7, A.8 and B.9.
A mortar is reported as located at C.29.d.2.8.

Machine Guns. Enemy machine guns were active during the night.
During the evening "Stand to" the ST. JEAN - WIELTJE ROAD was swept by bursts of machine gun fire.

Patrols. Three officers patrols were out during the night.
"A" went out at 10.15 p.m. from R.29 and returned by the same way at 12.30 a.m.
"B" went out at 10.40 p.m. at RAILWAY and re-entered at H.20.
"C" left C.29.a.30.15 at 10 p.m. and returned at 11 p.m.
All three patrols reported sounds as of working parties in the enemy trenches, but the moon being very bright, they could not move out very far.

INTELLIGENCE.

Enemy Movements. An enemy working party was seen opposite H.19/20 and dispersed by our Lewis Gun. They were apparently working on their wire.
Enemy is also reported to have been wiring at C.29.a.75.05. and Enemy in two's and three's were again seen at & (C.29.a.75.30 about C.30.b.25.15, moving South of GREY RUIN.

MISCELLANEOUS.

A hostile aeroplane dropped two bombs about 100 to 150 yards South of the MENIN ROAD between HELL FIRE CORNER and the Dump at about 9.45 p.m.

16th August, 1916.

Lieut-Colonel, G.S.,
29th Division.

D.S.118.

29TH DIVISION DAILY SUMMARY.

From 10 a.m. 14.8.16. to 10 a.m. 15.8.16.

OPERATIONS.

Artillery. During the day MUD LANE was shelled, but little damage done.
At 7.p.m. some shells were fired into RAILWAY WOOD but stopped when our guns retaliated.
WHITE CHATEAU was shelled at intervals with shrapnel, at 1.30.p.m. and at 9.30. with 5.9s.
At 5.30.p.m. and 7.30.p.m. H.E. were fired into POTIJZE.

Snipers. Snipers were active at 5.9. We retaliated with rifle grenades.

INTELLIGENCE.

Enemy Work. At 2.30.a.m. enemy working parties were observed opposite Nos. 1 and 2a Craters. They were fired on by Lewis Gun and disappeared.
The enemy were wiring opposite B.10 and working parties were heard during the night from I.5.b.4.7. to I.5.b.4.10. New sandbags are visible between these points.

Enemy Movements. At 2.p.m. two men were seen crawling in front of our wire at No.1 Crater. Bombs were thrown and the men disappeared.
Small bodies of men were observed at C.17.b.10.

MISCELLANEOUS.

Two objects as per sketch were observed about I.4.d.1.65. from I.4.d.1.65. on a bearing of 86° Magnetic

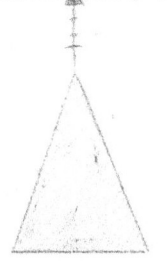 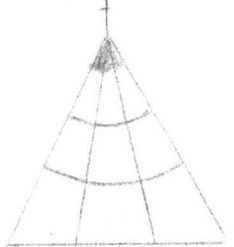

Several aeroplanes flew over our lines.
At 11.p.m. flashes apparently from an aeroplane were observed in the sky N.W. from A.8.

Major, G.S.
15th August 1916.   29th Division.

Intelligence,

VIIIth Corps.

Addendum to 29th Division Intelligence Summary - 15.8.16.

A report has been received that at about 1.20 a.m. 15th instant a hostile aeroplane appeared over the VLAMERTINGHE - POPERINGHE Road and fired a machine gun in bursts. It went away and at 2.40 a.m. appeared again dropping 5 bombs, afterwards it disappeared in a N.E. direction.

No damage was done.

One bomb fell at point H.2.d.9.1, near the 9.2" Howitzer Battery making a hole only a few inches deep.

15th August, 1916.

Major, G.S.,
29th Division.

D.S. 117.

29TH DIVISION DAILY SUMMARY.
From 10 a.m. 13.8.16. to 10 a.m. 14.8.16.

OPERATIONS.

Artillery. Enemy's artillery was very active during this period. From 6 p.m. to 9 p.m. about 160 5.9 and 4.2 H.E. shells were fired into POTIJZE.
MUDDY LANE, F.5, B.11, B.12, A.7, A.8, also received attention. YPRES was also shelled.

Machine Guns. Enemy machine guns fairly active during the night on A.6 and A.7.

Patrols. A patrol of the 2nd Royal Fusiliers went out from C.29.c.5.2 at 10.30 p.m. and remained out for 45 minutes. A disused trench was found at C.29.a.3.4 about 20 yards from our wire. This is blown in in many places and a number of enemy bombs were discovered, two of which were brought back. These are the usual enemy bombs, they were detonated and had the caps off ready for throwing.
An officers patrol went out from our right sector to examine ground on our right. They found an old Canadian communication trench but this was very badly cut up by shell holes. Old bits of barbed wire and other debris were lying about. Most of the shell holes were partly filled with water. This patrol returned in the direction of crater 1A and entered it. They were bombed from the eastern edge of the crater and replied vigorously. No casualties on our side.

INTELLIGENCE.

Enemy Movements. An officer reconnoitred our wire from H.20 to Railway and reports at 11.30 p.m. there was a party of the enemy (about 8 strong) in NO MAN'S LAND 40 yards from our wire. They withdrew to their own trenches.

Enemy Work. Fresh wire has been put up at point 67 (I.12.c.). Wire here is very strong.
The pile of sandbags in Sap-head opposite No.2A crater increases every day. Possibly there is a mine shaft near this Sap.
Enemy's working party about 50 yards in front of No.1 crater was fired on by one of our Lewis Guns. It is aserted that at least 4 or 5 of the enemy were accounted for.
Small parties of the enemy were observed about C.17.b.1.0.
A working party was heard at WHITE COTTAGE about midnight.

Train Activity. A train was heard at 3 a.m. behind the enemy's line.

MISCELLANEOUS.

A searchlight was observed on our left flank in a northerly direction.
A mackintosh was seen flying as a flag from L.R.B. COTTAGE.
Pigeons. A pigeon was reported to have been seen flying in the direction of the enemy's lines on the morning of the 12th, crossing our line about A.4. Another pigeon was observed flying from the German lines in the direction of the southern corner of YPRES on the morning of the 13th.
Aeroplanes. Enemy aeroplanes have been busy, during the day four were over our line between 4 p.m. and 7 p.m.

Major, G.S.,

14.8.16.

29th Division.

D. S. 186

HEADQUARTERS.
29th DIVISION.
INTELLIGENCE.

No..........
Date..........

29TH DIVISION DAILY SUMMARY.
From 10 a.m. 12.8.16. to 10 a.m. 13.8.16.

OPERATIONS.

Artillery. Enemy's artillery has been active during this period. Our trenches MUDDY LANE, DUCK WALK and A.3, A.7, A.8 and NEW JOHN STREET received attention.
Cross Roads at ST. JEAN and also YPRES – POTIJZE ROAD were shelled with shrapnel at 9.45 p.m.
H.E. was fired into JOHN STREET at 9 a.m. this morning.

Machine Guns. Enemy's machine guns quieter than usual. Our machine guns fired on enemy Railway at night, the line being searched over distance of 200 yards.

Trench Mortars. Enemy's trench mortars active on our Right Sector.

Snipers. The sniper who has been active was observed at C.29.a.8.4., he was sniped at, and has not fired since.

INTELLIGENCE.

Enemy Work. The enemy were observed working in front of Craters Nos. 1 and 2a, and also on their wire at I.6.c.0.1, one German was hit.
From the right of the Right Sector a good view of enemy's defences about HOOGE is obtained. A great deal of work has been done, several successive lines being close together with a large amount of barbed wire in front of each. This appears to be a very strong REDOUBT.

Enemy Movements. A number of trains were heard and a good deal of singing and whistling also sounds of transport.

Two parties, one of 6, and one of 9 men, were seen to enter Cottage at I.6.b.3½.3½. They left shortly afterwards carrying bundles and going in a northerly direction (Time 3.30 p.m. and 3.45 p.m.) – A dump suspected here.

MISCELLANEOUS.

Several enemy aeroplanes flew above our lines during this period.

At 9.20 p.m. enemy sent up a purple flare, and at two other times a green and also a red – nothing happened.

Major, G.S.,
29th Division.

13th August, 1916.

HEADQUARTERS
29th DIVISION

29TH DIVISION DAILY SUMMARY.

From 10 a.m. 11.8.16. to 10 a.m. 12.8.16.

OPERATIONS.

Artillery. Enemy's artillery more active during the day. OUTPOST FARM and CROSS ROAD FARM received particular attention. Vicinity of LA BRIQUE was also shelled.
At 9.30 p.m. the Trench Mortar Battery of the left sector was shelled.
At 8 a.m. this morning after extraordinary quiet period of about 4 hours, the enemy opened fire on trench in RAILWAY WOOD with field guns and trench mortars doing some damage.

Machine Guns. The enemy's machine guns were active during the night fire being chiefly directed on the ROULERS Railway between HELL FIRE CORNER and WEST LANE Barricade.
Our own machine guns retaliated.

Trench Mortars. JOHN STREET was shelled with trench mortars during the night.

Patrols. Patrols went out last night from the 2nd Royal Fusiliers to observe working parties. 1st patrol left our line at 10.50 p.m. from A.8 and went towards KAISER BILL. They met with no opposition and discovered a covering party of the enemy. This patrol returned and reported and had the Lewis Gun turned on to the working party. The patrol went out again at 12.45 a.m. and found the covering party dispersed.

Snipers. Enemy's snipers active during the early morning. A direct hit was obtained early this morning on a German who was standing on the parapet.

INTELLIGENCE.

Enemy Work. Enemy was hard at work in trenches opposite I.12.c.9.1 during the whole night.
A wiring party was heard at I.12.a.0.8 and also one at WHITE COTTAGE.
Sounds of dumping iron were heard at the MOUND.
A working party of about 80 men working behind KAISER BILL were dispersed by our Lewis gun fire at 4.30 a.m. this morning. 6 men were seen to fall.
New sandbags are to be seen at KAISER BILL.
Machine gun emplacement located behind WHITE COTTAGE, probably in Sap C.29.a.4.6.

Enemy Movements. To the rear of the MOUND and in a N. direction to KAISER BILL, there must be a line very close to the front line as the noise is very distinct. The shunting of trucks was heard between C.29.d.4.2 and C.29.b.2.05. Transport (horse) was also heard in rear of the MOUND and KAISER BILL.
A working party of ours report that the drivers have been heard to speak English.

MISCELLANEOUS.

Signals. Flag at C.22.d.9.2. has been removed.

Major, G.S.,

12.8.16.   29th Division.

Official copy

D.S. 114

HEADQUARTERS,
29th DIVISION.
INTELLIGENCE.

No............
Date............

29TH DIVISION DAILY SUMMARY.

From 10 a.m. 10.8.16. to 10 a.m. 11.8.16.

OPERATIONS.

Artillery. Enemy artillery inactive. Little shelling in vicinity of CROSS ROAD FARM. 3 H.E. shells fell near OUTPOST FARM, also several trench mortar bombs at 10 p.m.

Machine Guns. Enemy's machine guns fired intermittently during the night.
Machine gun emplacement (supposed) at C.23.c.1.6.
Machine gun fire mostly along Railway near F.13.
Our own machine guns retaliated vigorously.

Snipers. Enemy's sniping was active especially during the first part of the night and early this morning.
The eastern end of STRAND and FLEET STREET is traversed by snipers at long range.

Enemy Patrol. At 1.30 a.m. this morning a party of about 10 - 12 Germans attempted to bomb our front line near GULLY FARM at I.5.d.6.2. One German entered our trench and was killed. An exchange of bombs took place and remainder of enemy retired without getting nearer to our line than the barbed wire, where they dropped several of their bombs when retiring. Our casualties were 1 officer and 1 Sergeant killed.

INTELLIGENCE.

Enemy Work. Enemy were heard wiring along front at approximately I.12.a.½.6.
Enemy during the night appeared to be working hard, wiring, hammering in stakes on our front of right sub-sector. Wiring was going on to the N. of WIELTJE (C.23.c) and at WHITE COTTAGE (C.29.a). Sounds of sawing wood, shouting and whistling were heard.

Enemy Movements. Light trolley heard opposite A.7 at 8.10 p.m. coming from S. towards KAISER BILL and leaving again at 9.15 p.m. and again at 11.55 p.m. and 2.45 a.m.
Enemy transport was heard last night and sounds of dumping, probably from UHLAN FARM (C.29.b central).
Transport was also heard opposite A.7 from direction of YPRES - ZONNEBEKE Road towards KAISER BILL on road to UHLAN FARM (C.29.b central) at 11.30 p.m. It appeared to move on a soft track and then drop on to a metalled road.

MISCELLANEOUS.

Signals. Flag visible in enemy trench at about C.29.d.4.55.

Aeroplanes. Enemy's aeroplanes were active over our line at 7.30 p.m. yesterday.

[signature] Major
for Lieut-Colonel, G.S.,
29th Division.

11th August, 1916.

D.S. 113.

29TH DIVISION DAILY SUMMARY.

From 10 a.m. 9.8.16. to 10 a.m. 10.8.16.

OPERATIONS.

Artillery. At 9 a.m. enemy was shelling the POTIJZE - YPRES Road, while motor ambulances were passing, with shrapnel.
A point just West of the dead end of the CANAL at I.1.b. was shelled periodically during the day with H.E. fired in salvos of four.
The VLAMERTINGHE - YPRES Road was shelled at about 9.15 p.m.

Sniping. Enemy sniping more active than usual.

Machine Guns. Enemy's machine guns were active between 10 p.m. and 11 p.m.

Trench Mortars. Our trench mortars fired about 20 rounds from RAILWAY WOOD during the night at enemy working party. It stopped them and caused very little retaliation, two trench mortar bombs and three rifle grenades being fired back at our lines.

INTELLIGENCE.

Enemy Movements. Sounds of enemy transport were heard behind their lines, also a train.

Enemy Work. Enemy was strengthening his wire at C.29.d.4.3 and I.5.b.55.35. Wiring was also going on opposite our left sub-sector.
Working parties were heard at ARGYLE FARM and WHITE COTTAGE.
The enemy were heard working at several places, it appears that they are building a Light Railway or are using a large amount of iron material behind their front line near EITEL FRITZ FARM (I.5.b.6.7). Noise of this kind is often heard near this point.

MISCELLANEOUS.

Aeroplanes. The enemy was active with anti-aircraft guns against our aeroplanes.
At about 6.30 p.m. an enemy plane was over the SALIENT.

Major, G.S.,
29th Division.

10th August, 1916.

D.S. 112.

29th DIVISION DAILY INTELLIGENCE SUMMARY.

From 10.a.m. 8.8.16 to 10.a.m. 9.8.16.

OPERATIONS.

GAS ATTACK. A separate report on the hostile gas attack last night is being forwarded.

Artillery. During the gas attack the enemy's artillery did little damage to our Left Sector, GARDEN STREET and the village of St.JEAN was shelled with shrapnel, also the WIELTJE ROAD, CROSS ROADS causing a few casualties, otherwise the shelling was normal. YPRES came in for some shelling this morning.

MACHINE GUNS. Machine Guns were quiet during the day but active at "Stand To" traversing the front line until the gas attack began. At 2.a.m. they again opened fire; on every occasion our machine and Lewis Guns retaliated.

TRENCH MORTARS. Trench Mortars are believed to fire from trench running from C.29.a.3.9½. to C.29.a.7½.5.
Enemy Minenwerfer fired on CAMBRIDGE ROAD and S 21 about 1730 - 1800. Ceased fire immediately on our artillery retaliating: our own firing during gas discharge.

AEROPLANES. Two hostile aeroplanes which crossed our lines between FENCHURCH STREET and DUKE STREET at 12.30 p.m. and 8.p.m respectively are reported not to have been fired at at all, though the latter was flying low. On the other hand at 6.30 p.m. a hostile aeroplane was driven back apparently by one of our aeroplanes and at 8.15 p.m. two hostile aeroplanes, one of which dropped a white flare, were heavily fired upon by our A.A.Guns both coming and going. They returned at 8.25p.m. and each dropped a white flare, and on being shelled retired. At 8.30 p.m. another aeroplane was driven off by our A.A.Guns.

SNIPERS. were particularly active after the gas attack.

INTELLIGENCE.

At 1.40 p.m. two men in dark clothes were seen for a second or two at the head of the Sap at C.22.d.8½.4½ just North of the trees where the German flag is flying.

GAS SHELLS. Several dead rats have been found in the trenches in the area affected by the gas shelling of night of the 7/8th inst.
Flares were sent up in large numbers by the enemy during the gas discharge.
Wiring has been done by the enemy in front of their 2nd Line from about ~~I 6 a 60 to I 6 a 3.4~~.
I 6 a 60 to I 6 a 3.4.
The effect of the gas was felt at Divisional Headquarters.

Major G.S.

9th August, 1916.   29th Division.

D. S. 111.

29TH DIVISION DAILY INTELLIGENCE SUMMARY.

From 10 a.m. 7.8.16. to 10 a.m. 8.8.16.

ENEMY WORK.

New wire is reported at the following places :-
C.29.a.8½.4½, C.29.d.55 and C.22.d.9.9.

No work was seen to be in progress in the enemy's lines during the day, but our covering parties North and South of the ROULERS Railway heard work going on behind the enemy front line from 22.30 onwards during the night.

Our listening posts report sounds of talking and metallic clanging from the direction of C.29.a.6.8.

ENEMY MOVEMENT.

2 covered wagons proceeded from left to right on road behind GREY RUINS at 9 p.m.

MISCELLANEOUS.

About 11 p.m. some shells or rifle grenades containing gas were fired by the enemy from approximately I.5.b.8.7. Similar shells landed in I.4.b.9.0 to C.28.d.9.1. Full force of the effect was felt at 12.55 a.m. when a wiring party had to disperse. The smell of gas was noticeable until 1.35 a.m.

A copy of report from 1st Battalion Royal Inniskilling Fusiliers is attached and portions of the shells sent herewith for inspection.

Captain, G.S.,

8.8.16.

29th Division.

Special report on shells used by the enemy at 23.00 (and in the Intelligence Report of the 8th August, wrongly described as Rifle Grenades).

Herewith for inspection.

(a) Nose cap of Shell marked L.W.M.Z. with time fuse scale.

(b) Base of shell shewing four cylinders at base then a chamber filled with a white substance and next a lead chamber filled with a mustard coloured substance.

(c) Metal collar with part of the outer case attached.

(d) Part of thin (lead ?) inner case.

(e) Part of inner case with white enamel like substance attached.

(f) Part of inner case with loose white substance like chalk (as it was found).

(g) Part of circular metal collar.

(h) Circular piece of inner tubing with the white enamel like substance attached.

A further search will be made and a whole shell procured if possible.

The shells were apparently fired from some engine like a Stokes gun or rifle grenade stand. In some cases 4 appeared to be fired simultaneously. Their flight could be detected from the very start and their course followed through the air as they appeared to have a luminous tail like a comet. Their course was very high and like the flight of a rifle grenade.
When the shells were fired the noise was hardly audible, though the engine was apparently in the Enemy's front trench. When the shells burst there was a very slight detonation. The gas seemed in many cases not to be formed until some time after the shells had exploded and even today when the shells were dug up there was quantities of the mustard coloured substance which still appeared to ~~goxupwardsxand this~~ be evaporating.
On observation the fumes appeared to go upwards and this was corroborated by the fact that these shells if they fell on the sides of the trench did not harm the soldiers in the dug-outs close by or under the parapet.

EFFECT. The gas not only affected the eyes but also the throats of the men near and made them feel sick, so far as is known no one paraded sick today from the effects of the fumes.
Sentries were posted near where the shells fell they wore their gas helmets and felt no bad effects whatever, and as the bombardment lasted some time the helmets are probably an adequate protection.
The position of the shell was approximately C,5.a.2.9 and the place where another shell buried itself has been marked for inspection if desirable.

(Signed) HARDRESS LLOYD, Major,
Commanding 1st Royal Innis. Fus.

D.S. 110.

29th Division Daily Intelligence Summary.

From 10 a.m. 6/8/16 to 10 a.m. 7/8/16.

ENEMY WORK.

Men were loading and carting hay near GREY RUINS.
All through the night enemy working parties were heard along the front opposite FENCHURCH STREET to DUKE STREET, talking, singing and hammering: wheels running on trench tramway further back could be heard.

ENEMY MOVEMENTS.

Train observed on ROULERS railway at 8-45 p.m. last night in direction of D 21 d 6.5.

PATROLS.

1. Under Lt. Pritchard examined "no man's land" between points 59 and 67 and found ground much torn up by shells and long grass full of loose wire which much impedes progress. Enemy very alert, firing a machine gun on patrol repeatedly.

2. Under 2nd/Lt. Goold examined old firing line our left to railway line and ground in front. Found old fire trench obliterated, wire in front in good condition, not many shells holes in this part of "no man's land".
Strong enemy working party were out wiring. Flares sent up to-night and left came from support trenches.

3. Under 2nd/Lt. Ramsden went out to examine old firing line from N of Forester's Lane but was unable to enter it, as enemy had a bombing party in it

MISCELLANEOUS.

At 10.a.m. this morning a German flag was observed to be flying on the top of a tree at approximately C.22.d.9.2.
Over a dozen of our machines at 7.45 p.m. from enemy's lines appeared to drop smoke bombs or to have these fired at them. They burst about 200' under the planes and emitted huge volums of yellow smoke which formed a long broad descending ribbon about 150 to 200' long.

7th August, 1916.

Captain, G.S.
29th Division.

D.S. 109.

29TH DIVISION DAILY INTELLIGENCE SUMMARY.

From 10 a.m. 5.8.16. to 10 a.m. 6.8.16.

ENEMY WORK.

Work is done every night in Sap opposite Crater 2A.

Work has also been done on communication trench leading back from I.12.a.3.4.

The enemy was heard driving in stakes near L.R.B. COTTAGE. He also was working near KAISER BILL (C.29.cent.), whence came sounds of wheels on tram-rails.

ENEMY MOVEMENTS.

At 0230 a train was heard on YPRES - ROULERS Railway, also at midnight going away again at 0100.

Enemy transport was heard behind enemy's line at 2330 and again between 0200 and 0330.

MISCELLANEOUS.

At 2100 a light was dropped from an aeroplane.

At 8.30 this morning enemy biplane dropped white flares; it is not known with what design.

A pigeon was observed to rise from behind OUTPOST BUILDINGS (C.29.d.) at 7 p.m. and fly across our line at A.7.12. thereafter taking a course of 260° Magnetic.

Captain, G.S.,

6.8.16.   29th Division.

D.S. 108

29TH DIVISION DAILY INTELLIGENCE SUMMARY.

From 10 a.m. 4.8.16. to 10 a.m. 5.8.16.

HEADQUARTERS.
29TH DIVISION.
INTELLIGENCE.

No.............
Date............

ENEMY WORK.

Work was heard in sap-head opposite No.2A Crater last night. The party was fired on and twice stopped temporarily. This sap now reaches to within about 40 yards of Crater No. 2a and at its head, there is a high wall of sandbags.
Between 2300 and 0030 an enemy working party was heard wiring to right of Crater No. 6 at I.6.c.1.1.
Between 0000 and 0100 enemy was also hard at work in front line trench at I.5.d.
During the night the enemy was working in his front trenches between the MOUND and the VERLORENHOEK ROAD.
He also worked a short distance north of the SALIENT in C.29.central.
Posts were dug into the ground near L.R.B. COTTAGE.

ENEMY MOVEMENTS.

Horse transport was heard at 11.15 p.m. and 0300 directly in front of Crater No. 6.
At 7.40 p.m. one horse transport wagon was observed on road at D.23.d.2½.7.
Sounds of transport were estimated to come from the road at C.23.c.9.5½.
At 0845 a train was observed for 5 minutes at D.25.d.5.0 and then went off in direction of D.26.c.3.4.

MISCELLANEOUS.

A structure, very probably a machine gun emplacement, is visible in the parapet of the enemy's front trench at 62° (Magnetic) from C.28.a.70.63.
Snipers post has been located and appears to be at I.11.b.9.5.
At stand to in the evening, two green lights were dropped by an aeroplane over our line. No anti-aircraft guns were in action and it is not known that the aeroplane was hostile.
At 0400 a white disc was seen to be making signals. This continued intermittently until 0800. It is in German front line trench by OSKAR FARM. No action by the enemy followed the signals.

5th August, 1916.

Captain, G.S.,
29th Division.

D.S. 107.

29TH DIVISION DAILY INTELLIGENCE SUMMARY.
From 10 a.m. 3.8.16. to 10 a.m. 4.8.16.

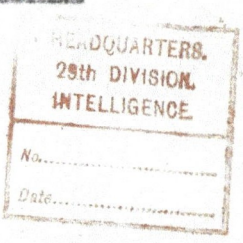

ENEMY WORK.

The enemy was heard driving in stakes near his front line at about I.6.c.1.8.

Fresh wire has been erected between WELL COTTAGE and C.23.c.6.7.

A structure, possibly a new sniper's post, is visible at C.23.c.3.2 and new work has been done at C.23.c.3.5 (Reported by "A" Coy. 2nd S.W.Bs.)

ENEMY MOVEMENTS.

The enemy was using his Trench Tram-lines opposite front C.29 during the night.

MISCELLANEOUS.

A hostile aeroplane, at 7.30 p.m. dropped several white lights. No result was observed to follow.

A Post is now established by us at Crater 1A, day and night. There are now two saps leading to it.

4th August, 1916.

Captain, G.S.,
29th Division.

D.S. 106.

29th Division Daily Intelligence Summary.

From 12 noon 2.8.16. to 12 noon 3.8.16.

ENEMY WORK.

A mound of earth at I.5.b.85.10 appears to have been enlarged since yesterday and is believed to be a sniping post.
Sap head opposite crater 2A has been strongly wired apparently prepared for defence.
During the night the enemy was heard wiring in the direction of L.R.B. Cottage, and working in the Sap about C.29.a.2.8 (Reported by 2nd S.W.B. patrol out in front of WIELTJE SALIENT from 10.30 p.m. to 1.30 a.m.)
He also worked on the MOUND where sounds of timber being handled could be heard.
Wire at C.29.a.6.5½ seems to have been strengthened with large coils.

MACHINE GUN EMPLACEMENTS.

A machine gun emplacement is strongly suspected at C.29.a.4.5½.

ENEMY MOVEMENTS.

Single men are often observed coming from WILDE Cottage at different times of the day and disappearing into trench near by.

3rd August, 1916.

Captain, G.S.,
29th Division.

D.S.105.

29TH DIVISION.
DAILY INTELLIGENCE SUMMARY.

From 12 noon 1.8.16. to 12 noon 2.8.16.

WORK.
Stakes were heard being driven in during the night at different points in the enemy's line opposite the Right (South) Brigade front, and also at about C.29.a.3½.5½. Fresh earth appears daily at I.5.b.5.4.

MOVEMENTS.
5 of the enemy were seen cutting crops at 6.15 p.m. at a point 95° (Magnetic) from C.28.c.6½.6½.

MACHINE GUN Emplacements are reported at C.29.a.5.6.
C.23.c.2½.½.
C.22.b.8.0.

A machine gun fired at our aeroplanes from a point 92° (Magnetic) from C.28.c.6½.6½.

TRENCH MORTARS. A trench mortar fired at C.28.b.8½.4½ between 8 a.m. and 10 a.m. from the direction of C.29.a.5.6.

Rifle Grenades were fired at C.29.a.3.2½.

D. Wyngham
Captain, G.S.,
29th Division.

2.8.16.

29th DIVISION.

Intelligence Summary - 1st August, 1916.

Enemy Work.

Work continues on dug-out at C.23.c.2.6. Enemy appears to be concreting rear wall of his trench for about 25 yards at this spot.
At C.23.c.3½.3½ two layers of new sandbags are visible and have been partially covered with fresh soil and timber is also visible.
New wire has been put out at I.5.b.8.X½ in front of main trench immediately south of mound AAA Two very distinct gaps can be seen about C.29.a.8½.4½.

Enemy Movements.

At 0500 a few Germans were seen digging and moving about in trench at I.5.d.9½.9.
Transport was heard, apparently on the ROULERS Road.
Several men were observed walking about near WILDE COTTAGE.
By the light of a flare, a German was seen standing by enemy sap at I.12.a.3½.0, in grey uniform and a cap with black peak and red band.
A relief appeared to be in progress in enemy front line between 0700 and 0800 at one point some men were seen moving along and as they passed another point, they waved their caps.

Miscellaneous.

At 2030 a cloud of thick white smoke was observed just behind German front line at OSKAR FARM.
At 0340 (31st ult.) two steel plates (about 2 feet sq.) were observed on parapet at C.23.c.3½.3½. One was taken down at 0350 and the other at 0410.

Captain, G.S.,

1.8.16.

29th Division.

W.R.17.

HEADQUARTERS.
29th DIVISION.
INTELLIGENCE.

No..................
Date................

29TH DIVISION WEEKLY OPERATIONS REPORT.

Period from 6 p.m. 3.8.16. to 6 p.m. 10.8.16.

OPERATIONS. The outstanding feature of the weeks operations was the hostile gas attack on our centre trenches on the night of the 8th/9th concerning which a full report has already been forwarded.

Artillery. The enemy's artillery has been generally active during the past week, the activity being rather more pronounced at the end of the week. The following have received most attention:- Trench H.15 to OUTPOST FARM, POTIJZE ROAD and WOOD, S.18, F.11, MUDDY LANE, KAAIE SALIENT and YPRES. GARDEN STREET, ST. JEAN, WIELTJE ROAD and CROSS ROADS were particularly shelled during the hostile gas attack on the night of 8th/9th.
Some gas shells or rifle grenades were fired at the trenches about the centre of our line on the night of 7th/8th, they affected the eyes and throat, but no casualties occurred.
Our artillery has retaliated vigorously on every occasion.

Machine Guns. The enemy's machine guns have been fairly active, more especially at night and at "Stand to" when they frequently traversed our parapet.
Our machine and Lewis guns have retaliated energetically, firing chiefly on the roads and dumps behind their line.

Trench Mortars. Hostile trench mortars have been active against our trenches between WIELTJE and WARWICK FARM, doing some damage to our trenches.

Rifle Grenades and Catapult bombs have been interchanged at intervals East of RAILWAY WOOD.

Patrols. Several officers patrols have reconnoitred NO MANS LAND and the German wire. They have ascertained that between points I.12.c.59 and 67 the ground is much torn up by shells and a mass of old wire. From No.4 Crater to RAILWAY Line, the old fire trench was found to be obliterated, the wire was in front in good condition, there were not many shell holes.
The enemy appears to be very much on the alert, and constantly sends up flares during the night.

Aeroplanes. Great aeroplane activity has taken place. Several German machines have been over our line, but have been kept at a considerable altitude by our anti-aircraft guns. The enemy have vigorously shelled our aeroplanes, and on one occasion they used a new variety of smoke shell which burst with a dense smoke cloud and fell like a curtain to the ground.

Snipers. Little sniping has taken place.

Major, G.S.,
10th August, 1916.   29th Division.

29TH DIVISION SUMMARY OF OPERATIONS.

Period 2.30 p.m. 31st July to 6 p.m. 3rd August, 1916.

The G.O.C. 29th Division took over command of the Right Sector of the Corps front at 2.30 p.m. on 31st July from G.O.C. 6th Division. The relief of the 6th Division by the 29th Division was completed on the night 1st/2nd August.

The period under review has been quiet.

OUR ARTILLERY. The 29th Divisional Artillery has been chiefly occupied in retaliation for enemy shelling and trench mortar fire, and in firing on isolated buildings within the enemy's lines: working parties have been dispersed and some points registered.

ENEMY'S ARTILLERY. The artillery of the enemy have not been particularly active. Crater 1A and MUDDY LANE have received the most attention. YPRES was mildly shelled on the morning of 3rd instant.

MACHINE GUNS. The enemy's machine guns have not been active on the whole. An emplacement is suspected at C.29.a.4.5½.

TRENCH MORTARS. The enemy's trench mortars have been active on A7, A8, B9 and B10, and SUNKEN ROAD. B10 was subjected to a fairly heavy bombardment and some damage was done.

SNIPERS. The enemy's snipers have been active from opposite RAILWAY WOOD, from KAISER BILL and from opposite WIELTJE.

Patrolling. Patrols have been out from our lines and have heard working parties in the enemy's lines and on his wire but have not encountered any hostile patrols.

Battle Casualties since the Division came into the line.

	Killed.	Wounded.	Missing.
Officers	-	1	-
Other Ranks	2	7	-

3.8.16.

Major-General,
Commanding 29th Division.

W.R.18.

29TH DIVISION WEEKLY SUMMARY. - OPERATIONS.

From 6 p.m. 10.8.16. to 6 p.m. 17.8.16.

HEADQUARTERS,
29th DIVISION,
GENERAL STAFF.

No.
Date.

ARTILLERY.
The enemy's artillery has been only normally active during the past week. Points which have received most attention are the following :- OUTPOST FARM and CROSS ROADS FARM, RAILWAY WOOD, POTIJZE, MUD LANE, NEW JOHN STREET.
Our artillery has always retaliated vigorously.

MACHINE GUNS.
The enemy's machine guns have again been active during the night, firing short bursts at selected points, principally along the railway between the WEST LANE barricade and HELL FIRE CORNER.
Our own guns have retaliated particularly vigorously lately firing at important points behind the enemy's line throughout the night.

TRENCH MORTARS.
The enemy have fired a good many T.M. bombs into our trenches particularly between WIELTJE and WARWICK FARM also into JOHN STREET. RAILWAY WOOD has also received some attention. Little damage has been done.

SNIPERS.
Up till yesterday the 16th instant, the enemy's snipers have been active more especially in the early morning, but yesterday they are reported to have been noticeably less active along our whole front.

PATROLS.
A hostile working party was observed by one of our patrols on the 11th/12th night, the patrol returned to our lines and had a Lewis Gun turned on the working party which was dispersed.
Another patrol discovered an old trench at C.29.a.3.4 with a great many German bombs in it, two of which were brought back.
A further patrol which went out from our extreme right returned by crater 1.A, they were bombed from the eastern edge of the crater and replied vigorously.
We had no casualties.

CASUALTIES.
A list of casualties for the week is subjoined

	KILLED.		WOUNDED.		MISSING.	
	Off.	O.R.	Off.	O.R.	Off.	O.R.
	3	2	1	68	-	-

D.Oky

Major, G.S.,
29th Division.

17.8.16.

29TH DIVISION WEEKLY OPERATION REPORT.

From 6 p.m. 17.8.16. to 6 p.m. 24.8.16.

ARTILLERY. The enemy's artillery fire has been normal during the last week: the following places received the most attention :- the WIELTJE - ST. JEAN - YPRES Road - New Trench at C.29.b. and CRUMP FARM.
In retaliation to our bombardment on August 21st, the enemy replied fairly vigorously on our front trenches both with artillery and trench mortars, the latter proving most destructive and flattening out a considerable portion of the trenches between NEW JOHN STREET and the WIELTJE - FORTUIN Road.

MACHINE GUNS. Hostile machine guns were particularly active against WIELTJE, the WIELTJE - ST. JEAN Road, and the New Trench at C.29.b. Bursts were also fired at POTIJZE WOOD and Road.
Our machine guns have also fired a great many rounds every night at suspected ration dumps, cross roads, communication trenches, etc.

TRENCH MORTARS. The enemy's trench mortars have not been so active as usual this week, and, except in retaliation for our bombardment on the 21st instant, have fired exceptionally few bombs.

SNIPERS. Hostile snipers have given little trouble lately, but the enemy have been firing occasional rounds, probably from fixed rifles, at certain points behind our line, they have done no damage.

PATROLS. We have sent out many patrols during the week, most of whom report the enemy working on their front trenches and wire opposite the whole of our front, more especially at the MOUND. One patrol reported having heard the sounds of iron being dumped probably at OSKAR FARM. No hostile patrols have been seen.

CASUALTIES. The following is a list of casualties for the week :-

KILLED.		WOUNDED.		MISSING.	
Off.	O.R.	Off.	O.R.	Off.	O.R.
2	12	4	52	-	-

24th August, 1916.

Major, G.S.,
29th Division.

29TH DIVISION WEEKLY OPERATION REPORT.

From 6 p.m. 24.8.16. to 6 p.m. 31.8.16.

ARTILLERY. 1. On the whole the enemy's artillery has been considerably less active than usual during the past week. His retaliation to our shelling has been feeble, and he has confined himself to occasionally shelling a few of our main trenches mainly with shrapnel. The following places received the most attention - POTIJZE Village, MONMOUTH TRENCH, POTIJZE ROAD, X.8 (where there were a few casualties) and RAILWAY WOOD.

MACHINE GUNS. 2. The enemy has been rather more than usually active with his machine guns lately. He has constantly swept WIELTJE and the WIELTJE - ST. JEAN ROAD at night.
Our guns have fired a great many rounds on various communication trenches, tramways, and important points behind the enemy's lines. Our Lewis guns have also been active. On one occasion it is believed that we killed 5 of a hostile working party.

TRENCH MORTARS. 3. Very little activity on either side.

PATROLS. 4. We have sent out several patrols during the week. The following facts have been established :-
    (a) The enemy does practically no patrol work, only one hostile patrol having been encountered.
    (b) Work has been proceeding nightly about OSKAR FARM.
    (c) Wiring has been continued at certain points along the enemy's front.
    (d) Two hostile machine guns have been approximately located.
    (e) An identification was obtained by the recovery of a dead German from a shell hole at C.28.b.60.88. He belonged to the 236th R.I.R.

CASUALTIES. 5. A List of Casualties during the week is subjoined.

KILLED.		WOUNDED.		MISSING.	
Off.	O.R.	Off.	O.R.	Off.	O.R.
-	4	1	52	-	-

Major, G.S.,
29th Division.

31.8.16.

www.ingramcontent.com/pod-product-compliance
Lightning Source LLC
Chambersburg PA
CBHW081546160426
43191CB00011B/1852